THEY SIGNED FOR US
by Merle Sinclair
and Annabel Douglas McArthur

From the Authors' Foreword:

ALMOST every citizen of the United States knows about the Declaration of Independence, the greatest statement of democratic rights and principles in history.

Curious, then, is the fact that most of us freedom-blest Americans cannot name half a dozen of the fifty-six patriots who signed the Declaration in Philadelphia that eventful summer of 1776.

How many Signers can you name?

"I thought I had remembered nine," confessed a man with a Ph.D. degree, who holds an important position with our government. "But

They Signed for Us

They Signed for Us

by

MERLE SINCLAIR

and

ANNABEL DOUGLAS McARTHUR

DUELL, SLOAN AND PEARCE

New York

Copyright © 1957 by Duell, Sloan & Pearce, Inc.

Library of Congress Catalog Card No.: 57-11062

First edition

Contents

Contents

Foreword

ALMOST every citizen of the United States knows about the Declaration of Independence, the greatest statement of democratic rights and principles in history.

Curious, then, is the fact that most of us freedom-blest Americans cannot name half a dozen of the fifty-six patriots who signed the Declaration in Philadelphia that eventful summer of 1776.

How many Signers can you name?

"I thought I had remembered nine," ruefully confessed a man with a Ph.D. degree, who holds an important position with our government. "But when I checked, I found only six were right."

The proprietor of a bookstore said she would have a hard time naming any besides George Washington and Patrick Henry. She was chagrined to learn that neither Washington nor Henry signed.

Who were the Signers? The least we, their beneficiaries, can do is to learn their names. The highest tribute we can pay these men is to cherish the freedom for which they risked their lives and fortunes, and to defend that freedom against every threat.

What sort of men were the patriots who risked a hangman's noose? What consequences did they suffer as a result of their bold and hazardous act?

To answer these questions, and to acknowledge a debt which we, in common with our fellow Americans, owe the sturdy heroes of '76, we have written *They Signed for Us*.

MERLE SINCLAIR

ANNABEL DOUGLAS MCARTHUR

Milwaukee, Wisconsin

Chronology

1774

SEPTEMBER 5—First Continental Congress at Philadelphia, Pennsylvania

1775

APRIL 19—Battles of Lexington and Concord, Massachusetts

MAY 10—Second Continental Congress at Philadelphia

1776

JUNE 7—Richard Henry Lee's Resolution for Independence introduced in Congress

JULY 2—Resolution for Independence passed by Congress

JULY 4—Declaration of Independence agreed to by Congress

AUGUST 2—Declaration of Independence signed

AUGUST 27—American defeat at Battle of Long Island, New York

DECEMBER 25—American victory at Trenton, New Jersey

1777

SEPTEMBER 27—Occupation of Philadelphia by the British

OCTOBER 17—Surrender of Burgoyne at Saratoga, New York

1780

MAY 12—British victory at Charleston, South Carolina

1781

OCTOBER 19—Surrender of Cornwallis at Yorktown, Virginia

They Signed for Us

They Signed for Us

THOMAS MC KEAN
Delaware

BENJAMIN FRANKLIN
Pennsylvania

THOMAS JEFFERSON
Virginia

BENJAMIN HARRISON
Virginia

CAESAR RODNEY
Delaware

O N E

"We Must Be Unanimous"

WHEN Thomas McKean, of Delaware, arrived at the
State House in Philadelphia that rainy Tuesday, July 2,
1776, his immediate concern was for his colleague,
Caesar Rodney. Would the ailing Rodney be able to
attend the day's crucial session of the Continental
Congress? Would he make it in time to break Delaware's
deadlocked vote?

The resolution coming up this morning—the most
important ever presented in the history of the thirteen
American colonies—proclaimed them independent of
Great Britain!

Rodney had been absent from Congress in an effort to
squelch a Loyalist uprising that threatened his home
territory. He must have been dead tired when he returned to his plantation near Dover last night. Maybe
he was too sick to comply with McKean's urgent message: "Get to Philadelphia at the earliest possible moment." Dover was eighty miles away.

During yesterday's debate on the resolution—as heated
as the weather attending it—McKean sensed an emergency. Always the man of action, he strode from the
Assembly chamber to take matters into his own hands.
He scribbled a note to Rodney. Then he hunted up an

express rider and told him to speed with it to Dover. He paid the messenger from his own purse.

On June 7, the resolution of Richard Henry Lee, delegate from Virginia, had been introduced in Congress. Lee, acting upon instructions from his provincial government, proposed:

That these United Colonies are, and of right ought to be, free and independent States, that they are absolved from all allegiance to the British Crown, and that all political connection between them and the State of Great Britain is, and ought to be, totally dissolved.

From the first, a majority vote on Lee's resolution for Independence was practically assured. After several days' debate, final action was postponed until July 1. Excitement over the measure mounted, both in Congress and throughout the provinces. About a third of the colonists, from New Hampshire to Georgia, bitterly opposed this act of rebellion or regarded it with anxious doubt.

The number of delegates willing to vote yes gradually increased. Those masters of persuasion, John Adams and his cousin Samuel, of Massachusetts, with other patriot leaders, worked unrelentingly to convert the opposition and hearten the dubious. New York, Pennsylvania, and South Carolina offered the chief resistance.

It became more and more clear that no mere majority, but a unanimous vote, was imperative. Agreement was necessary to convince Great Britain, her watchful enemies, the divided colonists—and even some of the members of Congress themselves.

The colonies had sent delegations of varying sizes to represent them at Philadelphia. However, each colony had only one vote, determined by the majority within its delegation.

Delaware had three representatives. McKean and Rodney vigorously supported Lee's resolution. The more moderate and cautious George Read felt the move premature. He would vote no today. If Rodney didn't arrive, Delaware's deadlocked vote would be thrown out.

Delegates had worked feverishly through the night to line up support for the resolution or to make a last-ditch stand against it. This morning the word was that Pennsylvania and South Carolina had capitulated to the patriot cause. The New York position looked favorable.

That left Delaware. Now, on this morning of July 2, it seemed to McKean that the fate of the resolution rested on one sick man—and he was not even in Philadelphia!

An alarming dispatch had been read in Congress before Monday's session ended, which helped wavering members to decide in favor of separation from King George III and his domineering ministers. It came from General George Washington, commander in chief of the Continental Army, stationed at New York with his pitifully small forces.

Washington reported that British vessels were appearing in New York harbor by threes and fours, that attack was imminent, that all his meager resources would be required to prevent disaster.

Rodney would be anguished, indeed, if Delaware failed the cause of Independence, all on account of him. He had served his province for more than twenty years, and was a recognized leader in the movement to rescue Delaware from British rule.

If Rodney reached Philadelphia in time to vote, it meant spending the night in his saddle, braving thunder gusts and mud. Such a trip was a great deal to expect of anyone, particularly a man in Rodney's condition. The forty-eight-year-old bachelor suffered grievously from a malignancy that had spread over half his face. Physicians had advised him to seek treatment in Europe, but he refused to leave the colonies in their crisis. His humor and a certain inward fire seemed to keep him going.

McKean himself, an outstanding lawyer, had long been a champion of colonial rights and felt strongly that the patriots should, as he put it, "stop talking and act." It was heartbreaking for him to contemplate Delaware as failing today.

Philadelphia, metropolis of the colonies with a population of almost 35,000, was the logical meeting place for the Continental Congress. Delegates to the First Congress had turned down an invitation to meet in Pennsylvania's State House in September, 1774, in favor of Carpenter's Hall, two blocks to the east. But the

Second Congress, convening in May, 1775, accepted the use of the Assembly chamber. The provincial government graciously retired to smaller quarters in the building.

The State House was a handsome two-story brick structure, set back about thirty feet from the south side of Chestnut Street, between Fifth and Sixth Streets. It had a hundred-foot frontage, with brick arcades connecting it to fifty-foot wings. In its tall steeple hung a great bell with an inscription from Leviticus:

Proclaim liberty throughout all the land unto all the inhabitants thereof.

Two chambers in the main structure, one for the Assembly and the other for the Supreme Court of Pennsylvania, were separated by a central hall about twenty feet wide. The Assembly chamber, where Congress met, was on the east side of the hall.

It was a little cooler this morning after the storm; but the atmosphere was humid, and heavy rain clouds appeared ready to break loose again. The thermometer hovered around 78 degrees. Delegates were arriving by carriage, on horseback, or afoot, and gathering in earnest little groups.

Pennsylvania's representation included that amiable genius, Dr. Benjamin Franklin, who, at seventy, was the oldest of the few old men in Congress.

Somber-suited Samuel Adams didn't look as if he had much in common with his fellow delegate from Massachusetts, the rich and elegant John Hancock. The bond between these two close friends was their fervent patriotism, their love of liberty. The British had been trying to apprehend these rebels ever since an unsuccessful attempt at Lexington fourteen months before. George III was offering £500 apiece for their capture. If caught, Hancock and Adams would be sent to England on charges of treason.

Thomas Jefferson was a member of the Virginia delegation. At thirty-three, he'd had quite an honor thrust upon him. He had been chosen to draft a declaration to the world of the colonies' claim to Independence, to be broadcast in the event Lee's resolution carried. He had been more than busy at it these recent weeks.

Everybody liked the tall, freckled, sandy-haired Jefferson. He was quiet and shy until one got to know him— and such a poor speaker that he hadn't attempted a single speech in his year in Congress. But he was an earnest worker in committee, and truly a master of the written word.

McKean, a tall, vigorous man, was pacing the hall or peering up Chestnut Street from one of the tall windows when he wasn't greeting his fellow congressmen. He knew that proceedings would start in a few minutes.

There was a dais, flanked by two fireplaces, in the

center of the east wall of the Assembly chamber. The presiding officer's desk and red-upholstered chair occupied this platform. Now John Hancock, handsome president of Congress, impressive as always in tiewig and ruffled stock, was taking his seat. Charles Thomson, secretary, sat at a desk just below him.

Through the open window there came the sound of horse's hoofs on rough cobblestones. McKean hurried to the entrance. Galloping up Chestnut Street, with his three-cornered hat awry, came Caesar Rodney! The tall, gaunt rider, mud-splattered and bedraggled, reined in his horse and slid from his saddle. Fatigue and suffering showed in every line.

McKean greeted him with fervor. Rodney had left Dover astride a swift horse, in a blinding thunderstorm, within ten minutes after receiving McKean's message. He had ridden the night through, supplied with fresh horses along the way. Still shod in boots and spurs, Rodney walked arm in arm with his fellow delegate into the Assembly chamber. The two were almost the last to be seated.

President Hancock called the session to order at once.

During the trying days of debate over Lee's resolution, Congress resolved itself into a Committee of the Whole to consider the measure. Each morning Hancock would relinquish the chair to Benjamin Harrison, huge and jovial member from Virginia, who was named chairman of this committee. At the end of the day, with

Hancock again presiding, Harrison would make the official report to Congress of the committee's deliberations. Today President Hancock called on Harrison for his final report before the vote. Presently the poll of the thirteen colonies began.

Two Pennsylvanians who couldn't bring themselves to vote yes had delicately stayed clear of the State House this morning, enabling their delegation to cast an affirmative vote. New York abstained from voting. Hourly, its delegates had awaited fresh instructions from the newly elected provincial convention. Their present orders restrained them from voting for drastic action. South Carolina, in a real spirit of co-operation, gave in for the sake of unanimity.

When Delaware was called, Caesar Rodney pulled himself to his feet. He said, "As I believe the voice of my constituents and of all sensible and honest men is in favor of Independence, and my own judgment concurs, I vote for Independence!" Then he sank exhausted to his seat.

The twelve colonies participating had voted unanimously for Freedom! Each man present fully realized what his vote meant in terms of personal danger should this rebellion fail. King George III had declared every rebel in the land a traitor. The penalty for treason was death by hanging.

They Signed for Us

John Adams	JOHN ADAMS *Massachusetts*
Saml Adams	SAMUEL ADAMS *Massachusetts*
Robt Treat Paine	ROBERT TREAT PAINE *Massachusetts*
Elbridge Gerry	ELBRIDGE GERRY *Massachusetts*
Richard Henry Lee	RICHARD HENRY LEE *Virginia*
Francis Lightfoot Lee	FRANCIS LIGHTFOOT LEE *Virginia*
George Wythe	GEORGE WYTHE *Virginia*

T W O

"The Causes Which Impel Them"

JOHN ADAMS claimed that events which resulted in the American Revolution began in 1760, when Britain defeated France and George III became King. With a war to pay for and an enlarged empire to protect, the mother country needed funds desperately. She expected her colonies to contribute to her treasury.

The Americans had tasted freedom, and they resented the taxes and controls which the British Parliament imposed. For the seeds of Independence were sown long before 1760—probably when the first colonies came to America, where necessity bred self-reliance.

The habit of independent thinking grew with each generation, and the *right* to think freely was more and more taken for granted. The spirit of liberty was bred into John Adams, one of a long line of New England individualists. He was a great-great-great-grandson of independent Priscilla of Plymouth Colony and the shy fellow she chided for not asserting *his* rights! With no heart for marrying the widower Standish, who sent John Alden to plead his cause, the young lady asked, "Why don't you speak for yourself, John?"

Patriot leaders realized that theirs was no mere revolt of American colonies from Britain, but a human revolution that had been centuries in the making. It was the protest of human beings against enslavement, against powers that sought to govern without consulting the governed.

The chief outrages imposed by the British were:

> The Writs of Assistance—search warrants issued by the courts.
>
> The Stamp Act—a tax affecting legal papers, newspapers, and ships' papers.
>
> The Townshend Acts, placing duties on imported articles, including tea.
>
> Interference in colonial governments.
>
> The quartering of British "redcoats" or "lobsterbacks" in Boston.
>
> The Boston Port Bill.

"Taxation without representation!" was the cry of the provinces. If Britain taxed them, why did they not have a voice in Parliament? Time after time, the colonists petitioned for a "redress of grievances," while earnestly declaring their allegiance to the King. Division grew between the Tories, who favored yielding to the mother country, and the Whigs, who supported the cause of liberty.

The Stamp Act prompted the organization of the Sons of Liberty, who included the more radical of the anti-

British elements. They became a strong and noisy force on the side of Independence. The Boston Port Bill of 1774 closed the port as punishment for the Boston Tea Party, the occasion when some of the radicals dumped 342 chests of tea into the harbor.

The port bill served to unite the colonies in a common cause. In distant Virginia, the House of Burgesses set apart the day on which the bill became effective as a time for fasting and prayer. The royal governor promptly dissolved the assembly. The burgesses then met at an inn and recommended an annual Congress of representatives from all the colonies. They appointed delegates; other colonies did likewise. Thus almost fifty members of the First Continental Congress were chosen to meet in September, 1774, at Philadelphia.

Delegates from Massachusetts included lawyer Robert Treat Paine; that honest, forthright man of law and order, John Adams; and his cousin Sam, rabble-rousing but high-minded Son of Liberty and member of the colony's House of Representatives. All were Harvard graduates.

Paine was more moderate than the Adamses. However, he was resolute in supporting Independence. He was to become General Washington's chief procurer of cannon and gunpowder.

Sam Adams made little money and dressed plainly. Before his departure for Philadelphia, anonymous friends equipped him with a new suit, hat, wig, silk hose, shoes, and a bit of cash.

Matters came to a crisis in Massachusetts in the fall of 1774. The House of Representatives defied the royal governor, formed itself into the first Provincial Congress, and elected John Hancock president. It appointed a Committee of Safety and voted to drill 12,000 Minutemen.

Hancock had received a fine inheritance from the merchant uncle who had taken him into his large commercial and shipping business. He went abroad for his uncle in 1760, and was in London when King George II died and George III, who would one day put a price on his head, became King of Britain. John was twenty-three that year.

Most wealthy, aristocratic Bostonians sided with the royal governors. But John Hancock was an enthusiastic supporter of the popular party. He was amazingly generous; though he lost much of his fortune in the Revolutionary War, he contributed about $100,000 to its prosecution.

The night of April 18, 1775, the British redcoats began their march from Boston toward Lexington and Concord. Their purpose was twofold: to seize the military stores at Concord and to capture patriots Hancock and Sam Adams.

That night the Committee of Safety met at Wetherby's Inn, about halfway between Boston and Lexington. It had word that several British officers were out searching for the two "traitors." Elbridge Gerry, a member of the committee, knew that Hancock and Adams were spending the night in Lexington, and sent them a warning.

Young Gerry planned to stay all night at Wetherby's Inn. In the small hours, the British troops advanced upon it. He escaped only by fleeing in his nightshirt to a neighboring cornfield.

Until he was thirty-seven, John Hancock was probably Boston's most eligible bachelor. Now he was engaged to marry beautiful Dorothy Quincy, and tonight the two were at dinner in the parsonage of the Reverend Jonas Clarke in Lexington. It was a house Hancock had enjoyed since childhood. His grandfather, the Reverend John Hancock, had occupied it for fifty-five years.

By midnight, all was dark and still at the parsonage. A sentry was posted outside. The silence was broken by a messenger on horseback galloping up to the door. The rider, out of breath, yelled, "Where's Mr. Hancock?"

"Don't make so much noise!" the sentry ordered sternly.

"Noise!" exploded Paul Revere. "You'll have noise enough before long. The Regulars are coming out!"

Hancock flung open his bedroom window. He called to Revere to come into the house. As he heard the news of the redcoats' approach, John Hancock's one thought was to dash to the village green to join the Minutemen who were mustering there. But the others persuaded him not to run any such risk of capture. He and Adams fled northeast toward the village of Woburn. As they departed Lexington, there came to their ears from the direction of the green the sound of the Minutemen's fife and drum.

Following defeat at Concord, the British offered pardon to all rebels who would return to their former allegiance—all except John Hancock and Samuel Adams. The two did not go back to Boston, but left on the long journey to Philadelphia for the meeting of the Second Continental Congress beginning May 10.

Just a month before, in March, 1775, a Virginia Convention had been held in St. John's Church, Richmond, out of reach of the royal governor at Williamsburg. George Washington, Thomas Jefferson, and Richard Henry Lee were among the distinguished Virginians present to hear fiery Patrick Henry say that war was inevitable unless the colonies gave in to a slavish role. As he urged military preparation, Henry spoke his most famous words, "Give me liberty or give me death!"

At that meeting, the tall, thin, aristocratic Lee also spoke with eloquence:

"We mean no aggression, no violence, no treason, but if the powers in England choose to regard this action as such, on them will fall the responsibility of the course taken by them.... If we have our disadvantages, so has England. It will put her to a vast disadvantage to have to transport over such a distance, in the contingency of war, her armies and supplies.... Admitting the probable calculations to be against us, I will say with our immortal bard:

> " 'Thrice is he armed that hath his quarrel just;
> And he but naked, though lock'd up in steel,
> Whose conscience with injustice is corrupted.' "

Washington, Henry, and Lee had all been delegates to the First Continental Congress the preceding fall. Three months after the Virginia Convention, young Jefferson departed for Philadelphia to replace another delegate in the Second Congress. He reached the city on June 20, "just in time to see George Washington set out for Cambridge to take command of the first American Army." Congress had made Washington commander in chief on June 15.

In another year, Patrick Henry would become the first governor of the sovereign state of Virginia.

Public opinion swerved noticeably toward Independence in the early months of 1776, strongly influenced by a pamphlet called *Common Sense*. It was written by journalist Thomas Paine, who called for immediate separation from Britain. More clearly than anyone else had done, Paine indicated that America could and should become the haven of free peoples.

Richard Henry Lee's role in the spring of '76 was that of spokesman for the Virginia delegation in Congress, which included his younger brother, Francis Lightfoot Lee. The two belonged to one of Virginia's most distinguished families. Francis was less colorful than Richard, but quite as ardent a patriot. He had served in the House of Burgesses since 1758, when he was twenty-four, until he came to Congress.

On May 15, the Virginia Convention at Williamsburg passed a resolution that the delegates at Philadelphia be instructed to propose to Congress that the colonies be declared free and independent states, absolved from all allegiance to the Crown or Parliament of Great Britain. This provincial resolution was read in Congress on May 27. It was tabled for ten days while the delegates attended to other matters. Then, on June 7, Richard Henry Lee rose to make his resolution, "That these United Colonies are, and of right ought to be, free . . ."

Before Lee had a chance to sit down, John Adams seconded the motion for Independence. A happy day in Adams' life! He had waited a long time for this moment.

In the discussion which followed, these two masters of debate, Lee and Adams, led the element favoring the resolution. They had the valuable support of one of the most influential Americans of that day, George Wythe of the Virginia delegation.

Wythe was a thinker, a scholar, a man of public affairs. He was to become America's first law professor, at the College of William and Mary in Williamsburg. Jefferson had studied under Wythe and admired him enormously. George Wythe had taken the stand that the only political link between the colonies and Great Britain was their common allegiance to the King; that "that nation and its Parliament had no more authority over us than we had over them."

One reluctant delegate was Virginia's Carter Braxton, who had more conservative views on how to deal with Britain. He had come to Congress in February, sent, it was said, by Virginians who were "so alarmed with the Idea of Independence that they have sent Mr. Braxton on purpose to turn the Vote of that Colony, if any Question on that Subject should come before Congress."

Many delegates merely regarded Lee's proposition as premature. Some felt they should have instructions from their provincial governments before voting on such a momentous measure. Final action was postponed several weeks.

To save time, in case the resolution passed, Congress appointed a committee of five to prepare a Declaration setting forth the principles involved: John Adams, Benjamin Franklin, Thomas Jefferson, Roger Sherman of Connecticut, and Robert Livingston of New York.

Jefferson was named because of his gift for writing, and because he had aroused no political antagonisms. The committee promptly made him the sole draftsman of the document.

He had simple lodgings, a second-floor parlor and bedroom, in the home of a Philadelphia bricklayer. Here he worked diligently for almost three weeks composing the Declaration, putting to use a portable writing desk he had invented. His task was to put down in sublime language the concepts of freedom to which he and his fellow citizens were devoted. These convictions were:

All men are equal in God's sight, though their talents, virtues, and circumstances of birth vary. They are born to equal rights in this world. These rights, being natural and not political, therefore are inalienable—incapable of being surrendered or transferred. No other man or group or nation is entitled to deprive any human being of such rights.

Jefferson showed his draft to Adams and Franklin, separately, before submitting it to the committee. They made a few minor changes. On June 28, the Friday before the vote on Lee's resolution came up, Jefferson submitted his final copy to Congress.

As soon as Lee's resolution was adopted on July 2, Congress took up debate on the Declaration. John Adams, of course, supported the document in masterful fashion, but the delegates on the whole were merciless critics. Propriety forbade Jefferson's defending his phrases. So he said nothing. But Dr. Franklin, sitting next to him, could tell that he was fairly writhing inside.

Actually, Jefferson's colleagues paid his composition enormous tribute by adopting it with no more changes than they made. They deleted only what they considered impolitic, then put the finishing touches to a trea-

tise of such grace and felicity as to become one of the
world's immortal documents.

*When in the Course of human events, it becomes
necessary for one people to dissolve the political bands
which have connected them with another, and to assume among the Powers of the earth, the separate and
equal station to which the Laws of Nature and of
Nature's God entitle them, a decent respect to the
opinions of mankind requires that they should declare
the causes which impel them to the separation.*

*We hold these truths to be self-evident, that all
men are created equal, that they are endowed by their
Creator with certain unalienable Rights, that among
these are Life, Liberty, and the pursuit of Happiness.
That to secure these rights, Governments are instituted
among Men, deriving their just powers from the consent of the governed. That whenever any Form of
Government becomes destructive of these ends, it is
the Right of the People to alter or to abolish it, and to
institute new Government, laying its foundation on
such principles and organizing its powers in such form,
as to them shall seem most likely to effect their Safety
and Happiness. Prudence, indeed, will dictate that
Governments long established should not be changed
for light and transient causes....*

By Wednesday night, July 3, the Congress was far
from agreed, and debate was held over until the next
day.

Thursday morning, July 4, was sunny and pleasant, with a breeze from the southeast. The temperature was 72 degrees when Congress convened at nine o'clock.

Soon after President Hancock opened the meeting, the body again resolved itself into a Committee of the Whole. Chairman Harrison presided. Controversy flared again, and went on and on into the afternoon. The air became close. Delegates grew weary wrestling with Jefferson's rhetoric.

"The debate seemed as though it would run on interminably," Jefferson wrote later. "The weather was oppressively warm and the room occupied by the delegates was hard by a livery stable ... the horse-flies swarmed thick and fierce, alighting on the legs of the members and biting hard through their thin silk stockings. Handkerchief in hand they lashed at the hungry pests to no avail."

Toward evening, Hancock resumed the chair. Harrison reported that the Committee of the Whole had agreed to a Declaration. The document was read once more. The vote for its adoption was taken without dissent.

The only Signer of the Declaration of Independence on July 4, 1776, was John Hancock, president, on behalf of the members of Congress. Charles Thomson, secretary, attested Hancock's signature.

Quickly, the tired delegates ordered that copies of the Declaration be printed that night—and that Independence be proclaimed in each of the *United States*.

CHAPTER

They Signed for Us

Oliver Wolcott	**OLIVER WOLCOTT** *Connecticut*
John Hancock	**JOHN HANCOCK** *Massachusetts*
Step. Hopkins	**STEPHEN HOPKINS** *Rhode Island*
William Ellery	**WILLIAM ELLERY** *Rhode Island*
Charles Carroll of Carrollton	**CHARLES CARROLL OF CARROLLTON** *Maryland*
Samuel Chase	**SAMUEL CHASE** *Maryland*
Wm. Paca	**WILLIAM PAÇA** *Maryland*
Thos. Stone	**THOMAS STONE** *Maryland*

THREE

"Proclaim Liberty . . ."

SUDDENLY, the big bell in the State House steeple pealed joyously. The appointed signal! Cheers rose from the waiting crowds.

"Proclaim liberty throughout all the land..."

Cannon boomed, drums rolled. Church bells rang, sounding the death knell of British domination!

News of the adoption of the Declaration of Independence spread like wildfire. Ready messengers leaped into their saddles to ride and spread the word. The Declaration had been ordered printed on a single large sheet, "45.5 x 37.5 cm." or approximately eighteen by fifteen inches. These broadsides were distributed with all possible speed, to be read in the provincial assemblies, pulpits, market places, and army camps.

On July 8, the Liberty Bell summoned citizens of Philadelphia to the State House yard for a public reading of the document. Colonel John Nixon mounted a high platform and spoke the noble lines in a strong, clear voice. The crowd, now hushed, listened intently throughout.

"... for the support of this Declaration, with a firm reliance on the protection of Divine Providence, we mutually pledge to each other our Lives, our Fortunes, and our sacred Honor."

Patriots shouted their approval of the pronouncement of their leaders. Some of them celebrated by tearing down the King's Arms over the seat of justice in the courtroom and casting such vestiges of authority into a bonfire in the street. Processions and demonstrations lasted till midnight, when thunder and lightning sent the excited townspeople running to their homes.

Newport, Williamsburg, Charleston—a great many cities and towns—held gay celebrations, and patriotic observances with speeches and prayers. Dover arranged a grand turtle feast. In Savannah, jubilant citizens burned King George in effigy, and conducted a mock funeral service over his grave.

Not even a smallpox epidemic kept a great crowd from assembling in Boston. The Declaration was read from a balcony of the Massachusetts State House. At a given signal, thirteen cannon boomed across the New England shore. Bostonians celebrated with banquets and bonfires, having special reason to rejoice over their freedom from Britain and her obnoxious redcoats. According to a Boston newspaper, "The King's Arms, and every sign with any resemblance of it . . . together with every sign that belonged to a Tory, was taken down and made a general conflagration of in King Street."

In New York, General Washington ordered that the Declaration be read at the head of each brigade of the army at six o'clock, the evening of July 9. The brigades were drawn up in hollow squares. Washington, mounted on his horse, took up his position within one of these squares while an aide read the broadside. Afterward, the commander in chief reported to Congress on "the expressions and behavior of officers and men testifying their warmest approbation of It."

Civilians rushed to Bowling Green, where stood a life-size equestrian statue of George III. They tore down the figure, which was made of lead, richly overlaid with gold. What fine ammunition it would make!

The metal was transported to the home of Brigadier General Oliver Wolcott, a Connecticut delegate to Congress. Behind his white house in Litchfield, the general's wife and children, assisted by several ladies of the village, melted down His Majesty into 42,088 bullets for the American army. Mary Ann Wolcott, eleven, with great industry made 10,790 of them. Her eight-year-old brother Frederick turned out 936 bullets. *Their* father was a general!

General Wolcott was a tall, distinguished-looking man of forty-nine, son of a former colonial governor and a lawyer in private life. After graduation from Yale at the head of his class, he became active in both military and legislative affairs.

Within weeks after the statue's commitment to the patriot side, Connecticut's governor and Council of Safety placed General Wolcott in command of fourteen regiments which were to march in response to Washington's urgent appeal for aid in the defense of New York. Wolcott, just recovered from an illness that brought him home from Philadelphia, wrote, "I shall most cheerfully render my country every service in my power."

Later, while participating in the battle with British General Burgoyne's forces at Saratoga, New York—so the story goes—General Wolcott, in his supply, came across some bullets of "melted majesty" that had been made at his Litchfield home.

On July 19, according to the secret domestic Journal of Congress, the Declaration of Independence was ordered engrossed on parchment and signed by the delegates.

The day of the Signing was August 2. As members gathered for this meaningful ceremony, William Ellery of Rhode Island—a witty, literary chap who wrote epigrams about his fellow delegates while they spoke in Congress—sought a spot where he could witness the signature of each man.

"I was determined," he said, "to see how they all looked as they signed what might be their death warrants. I placed myself beside the secretary, Charles Thomson, and eyed each closely as he affixed his name to the document. Undaunted resolution was displayed on every countenance."

John Hancock signed in large, shaded letters. His flowing handwriting was the result of long hours of practice in penmanship back at the Boston Latin School.

"There!" he declared. "John Bull can read my name without spectacles, and may now double his reward of £500 for my head. *That* is my defiance!"

Contrasting with Hancock's confident signature was the shaky scratch of Stephen Hopkins, Ellery's sole colleague from Rhode Island. Hopkins was the second oldest Signer, and suffered from palsy. As he handed the quill to Ellery, he said valiantly, "My hand trembles, but my heart does not!"

Hancock is reported to have said as others signed, "We must be unanimous. There must be no pulling different ways; we must all hang together."

"Yes," replied Dr. Franklin, "we must all hang together, or most assuredly we shall all hang separately."

Tradition also has it that Hancock turned to a new member from Maryland, Charles Carroll, and asked if he would sign. Carroll was one of the richest men in America. He had much to lose.

"Most willingly," he answered. Taking the pen, he wrote, "Charles Carroll of Carrollton." He was the only Signer to write anything more than his name. Carrollton was his magnificent estate, and he was in the habit of including its name in his signature to distinguish him from his father and another Carroll of the same name.

As he moved to his seat with the easy grace of the expert swordsman, one of the other delegates said in an aside, "There go a few millions!"

Carroll and the other men of Maryland—Samuel

Chase, William Paca, and Thomas Stone—felt a special risk in signing because their families and property were so vulnerably situated near the long, exposed coastline of the Chesapeake area, all patrolled by British ships.

The New Englanders considered the Maryland members unduly given to pleasure. But there was no doubting their devotion to Independence.

Carroll had been well educated in France and England. He was a talented political writer, and had become a strong influence through an anonymous newspaper discussion in which he signed himself "First Citizen." The provincial government, through the press, thanked the unknown author who so effectively opposed Britain's taxation of the colonies without their consent.

Carroll's father had given him the Manor of Carrollton, an estate of some 10,000 acres. He managed the family plantations and received an enormous income from loans, mortgages, and the sale of tobacco.

Though new as a delegate, Carroll was well known to Congress. In the spring he had been sent to Canada on a delicate political mission. The colonies hoped that their neighbor to the north could be persuaded to join the rebellion against the mother country—or, at least, to remain neutral.

In a letter, John Adams explained the choice of Carroll: "He speaks their language as easily as ours; and what is perhaps of more Consequence than all the rest, he was educated in the Roman Catholic Religion. . . . In the Cause of American Liberty his ... Fortitude and Perseverance have been so conspicuous that he is said to be marked out for peculiar Vengeance by the Friends of the Administration; but he continues to hazard his all, his immense Fortune, the largest in America, and his life."

Carroll was accompanied by the diplomatic Franklin and persuasive Samuel Chase. But their mission failed. Dr. Franklin became ill and returned early from Montreal. He reached Philadelphia in time to serve on the committee to draw up the Declaration. Carroll and Chase presented their written report to Congress on June 12. Then Carroll hastened to Annapolis, where instructions again had been issued to delegates in Congress to vote *against* Independence. He and Chase worked hard to get these orders reversed; and on June 28, the Friday before the vote, the Maryland delegation was empowered to join with a majority in favor of Lee's resolution.

Huge, boisterous Samuel Chase was a real contrast to the small-boned, gentlemanly Carroll. This son of an Anglican clergyman was nicknamed "Bacon Face" because of his fiery complexion. He practiced law, and had served in the Assembly of his province along with William Paca, his stanch friend of law-school days. The two began a long association in politics, fighting oppression wherever they found it and contributing to the general welfare. One time, at their own expense of nearly a thousand dollars, they supplied rifles to a volunteer corps.

Paca was a handsome, engaging fellow. He and his friend Chase were responsible for a considerable number of high jinks in the course of their careers. On one occasion, the two led a crowd of citizens in protest against a proclamation of the colonial governor.

They copied the edict on a large sheet of paper, formed a procession to a gallows they had erected at the edge of town, and delivered the offensive words to the gibbet. After allowing sufficient time for the proclamation's demise, they enclosed it in a small coffin they had brought along, and buried it beneath the gallows. Guns mounted on an elegant schooner belonging to Paca fired regularly during the obsequies.

The perpetrators marched in close order back to town and spent the remainder of the day in gala fashion.

The fourth Marylander, quiet thirty-three-year-old Thomas Stone, had no part in such pranks. Though a lawyer, too, he seldom spoke out even in Congressional debate. But his good sense and hard work made him a valuable member of important committees. He was a firm defender of colonial rights.

Several delegates who could not be present on August 2, including General Wolcott and Thomas McKean, who were both away with the army, signed the Declaration later. Because of changes in delegates between July 4 and August 2, not all who voted for Independence were privileged to sign; and a number of those who affixed their signatures were not members of Congress when the Declaration was agreed to.

For fear of serious reprisals against the Signers and their families, their names were not made public for six months.

They Signed for Us

PHILIP LIVINGSTON
New York

FRANCIS LEWIS
New York

WILLLIAM FLOYD
New York

LEWIS MORRIS
New York

JOHN HART
New Jersey

ABRAHAM CLARK
New Jersey

RICHARD STOCKTON
New Jersey

JOHN WITHERSPOON
New Jersey

FRANCIS HOPKINSON
New Jersey

FOUR

"Our Lives, Our Fortunes"

THE BRITISH now marked for special vengeance all members of Congress whom they suspected of having signed for Independence. Most of the delegates were busy in Philadelphia, leaving their families and property exposed to frenzied attacks by spiteful Loyalists who were aiding the enemy.

With the invading fleet already at their shores, the four New York delegates—Francis Lewis, William Floyd, Philip Livingston, and Lewis Morris—practically signed away their property when they put their names to the Declaration. This they knew, and they also felt the gravest concern for their families. These men were wealthy aristocrats, with luxurious town houses and country estates filled with attractive loot for plundering.

New York's Provincial Congress had moved to White Plains for safety, and on July 9 had received the Declaration. A resolution was adopted unanimously approving the Independence for which their delegates had been restrained from voting, and stating that the members of the New York Congress would "at the risk of our lives and fortunes, join with the other colonies in supporting it."

Late in August, the British and their mercenaries, the Hessians, were ready to pounce upon General Washington and his little army, gathered in slender forces to protect New York City against attack. On the twenty-seventh, enemy forces landed on the southwest shore of Long Island, about 25,000 strong. They advanced in three divisions, inflicting terrible losses upon the stubborn colonials. About one fifth of Washington's men were killed, wounded, or captured.

Following the Battle of Long Island, the commander in chief and his generals met in the elegant country house of Philip Livingston on Brooklyn Heights, and decided to evacuate. Leaving their campfires burning, the remnants of the American troops escaped by night across the river and took up a position on Harlem Heights.

A woman Loyalist sent her servant to warn the British, but he was seized by Hessian soldiers who understood only German. They detained the fellow until someone who spoke English could take his message. By that time, the Americans had retreated safely northward through the city of New York.

The conquering army swarmed over Long Island. They burned and plundered the home of Signer Francis Lewis at Whitestone, and carried off his wife as a prisoner. Mrs. Lewis was confined in a filthy barracks and treated with great brutality. She had no bed to lie on, and no change of clothing for months. This disgraceful treatment came to the attention of Congress. General Washington then arranged for her exchange for two women prisoners of the Americans.

Mrs. Lewis had suffered so severely that she never regained her health, and died two years later.

Francis Lewis was a merchant, born in Wales and educated in Scotland and England. His extensive travels had taken him twice to Russia. He early became one of the Sons of Liberty. At sixty-two, he was elected to Congress. His business acumen proved valuable to the committees on which he served.

William Floyd was practically ruined by the Revolution. He had participated in a move of resistance against British oppression that had developed in the eastern part of Long Island, where his home was located. He was sent to the First and the Second Continental Congress, and shared the difficult task of supplying the army.

Tories plundered Floyd's extensive woodlands until they were "despoiled of almost every thing but the naked soil." They took over the family home, appropriating farm implements, stock, and household goods, as Mrs. Floyd and the children escaped with other victims across Long Island Sound to Connecticut.

Floyd and his family were exiled from their home for seven years. He received no income from his property until after the treaty of peace was signed and the British evacuated in 1783.

Philip Livingston was literally "to the manor born." His grandfather once owned 160,000 acres along the east bank of the Hudson River, constituted under English law as the Manor of Livingston, in which the lord exercised his own jurisdiction. Philip went to Yale, and became a successful New York importer.

All his business interests, and his mansion on Duke Street, fell to the enemy. His country estate on Brooklyn Heights became a British naval hospital. Homeless, the members of his family fled up the Hudson to Kingston, New York. They were further endangered when the British burned Kingston.

Public-spirited and generous—one of a family that "had virtue and abilities as well as fortune"—Livingston sold some of his remaining property to help maintain the country's credit.

He never had a chance to return home. He died in 1778 while serving in Congress.

The family of Signer Lewis Morris also had to find refuge when the Manor of Morrisania in Westchester County was appropriated by the enemy. It was part of property known as Bronck's Land, named for its original owner, the first permanent settler of the county. The invaders destroyed valuable timber, crops, and gardens on the thousand-acre tract and drove away the livestock.

The Morrises, like the Floyds, were denied their home for seven years. Lewis Morris became a brigadier general of Westchester militia, and had three sons who served as officers in the American army.

Washington's defeat on Long Island was a harsh blow to the colonies. They began to realize what it would mean if they lost the war.

The American troops—some of the men barefoot in the snow—retreated across New Jersey. At times the pursuing British were so close that the van of the red-coats was within sight of Washington's rear guard.

The New Jersey Tories welcomed the British and Hessian forces, and aided them in tracking down the "traitors" who had signed the Declaration.

The enemy encamped at Trenton. Living near the town was "Honest John" Hart, one of the five New Jersey Signers. He had a large farm and several grist mills. Hart strongly resented British taxation, asserting that he felt himself a slave if taxed "to the value of a straw" without representation.

While his wife lay on her deathbed, Hessian soldiers descended upon Hart's property, damaging his mills and devastating his farmland. He was hunted like an escaped criminal as he fled through the woods, sleeping in caves or any haven he could find. One night Honest John was so hard pressed for a place of safety that he slept with a big dog.

By the time this sixty-five-year-old man could return to his scourged land, broken in health by anxiety and hardship, his wife had died. His thirteen children were scattered in every direction.

That strong-minded, heavy-browed Signer, Abraham Clark of New Jersey, had two officer sons in the army, who were captured and confined on a prison ship. Britain's prisons were loathsome enough; its prison ships were worse. They provided the cheapest means of disposing of prisoners because they died off so fast. On the *Jersey*, where the Clark boys were held, 11,000 American prisoners perished. New York harbor smelled of death.

The Clarks suffered special hardships because of their father's stand. But patriotism was strong in this plain and pious Signer, and he rejected the enemy's offer to free his sons if he would renounce his cause in favor of King and Parliament. One son was confined to a dungeon for a time, without food except the little his fellow prisoners could pass through a keyhole.

The lives of two New Jersey Signers, Richard Stockton and John Witherspoon, and that of Signer Benjamin Rush of Pennsylvania were associated in several ways. Judge Stockton, of the State Supreme Court, was a trustee of the College of New Jersey (later named Princeton). Ten years before the Signing, when Stockton and his family left for a visit to Scotland, the college trustees asked him to persuade the great Scottish preacher, Dr. John Witherspoon, to become president of the school.

The good doctor was willing, but his wife rebelled at living in the wilds of America. She was won over by a young American, Benjamin Rush, who was studying medicine in Scotland at the time.

Famous Dr. Witherspoon was a dignified Presbyterian who spoke eloquently from the pulpit with a strong Scottish accent. He became a great American, academically, ecclesiastically, and politically. During the Congressional debate over Independence, a dissenting delegate ventured that the colonies were not "ripe" for separation from Britain. Dr. Witherspoon rose to his great height and retorted, "In my judgment, sir, we are not only ripe, but rotting for the want of it!"

In January, 1776, the now famous Dr. Rush of Philadelphia married Richard Stockton's daughter Julie, with Dr. Witherspoon officiating. Within a few months, the minister, the father of the bride, and the bridegroom would all participate in another ceremony—the Signing of the Declaration.

When the British approached Princeton, President Witherspoon closed the college. The enemy billeted in Nassau Hall and destroyed the college library, which included hundreds of fine volumes that he had brought from abroad.

After signing on August 2, Judge Stockton went north to inspect Washington's army, then returned to Congress to give his report. From Philadelphia, he rushed to his home at Morven to rescue his wife and children.

The Stocktons took refuge with friends, but a Loyalist

betrayed their hiding place. In the night, the judge was dragged from bed and brutally treated, then thrown into prison. This distinguished jurist, who had worn the handsome robes of a colonial court, now shivered in a common jail, abused and all but starved.

A shocked Congress arranged for his parole. Invalided by the harsh treatment he had received, he returned to Morven to find his furniture and clothing burned, his fine horses stolen, and his library—one of the finest private collections in the country—completely destroyed. The hiding place of exquisite family silver, hastily buried, had been betrayed by a servant.

The Stocktons were so destitute that they had to accept charity. For the judge's fortune was gone, too. He had pledged it and his life to his country. He lost both. He did not live to see the Revolution won.

The fifth New Jersey Signer was a composer of popular songs! He was Francis Hopkinson, an animated little man, witty and versatile, who wrote the music for "My Days Have Been So Wondrous Free." He liked to doodle with his pencil when bored by long Congressional debates. He loved the pigeons he raised, and had a pet mouse—which he fed at the table!

This engaging fellow was a lawyer, statesman, churchman, writer, and inventor. He won great popularity with verse that satirized the British. In "The Battle of the Kegs," he ridiculed the alarm of the redcoats when the

Americans floated kegs of gunpowder down the Delaware River to annoy enemy ships.

The artistic Hopkinson is said to have helped design the American flag. It was his father, a prominent Philadelphia lawyer, who introduced Benjamin Franklin to the study of electricity.

Francis married Ann Borden (whose wealthy father founded Bordentown, New Jersey) and thus became the brother-in-law of Signer Thomas McKean, who married Ann's sister Mary.

The British ransacked the Hopkinson home at Bordentown.

CHAPTER

They Signed for Us

Rob Morris	**ROBERT MORRIS** *Pennsylvania*
Benjamin Rush	**BENJAMIN RUSH** *Pennsylvania*
Geo Clymer	**GEORGE CLYMER** *Pennsylvania*
Jas. Smith	**JAMES SMITH** *Pennsylvania*
Geo. Ross	**GEORGE ROSS** *Pennsylvania*
Geo Read	**GEORGE READ** *Delaware*
Geo. Taylor	**GEORGE TAYLOR** *Pennsylvania*
James Wilson	**JAMES WILSON** *Pennsylvania*
John Morton	**JOHN MORTON** *Pennsylvania*

FIVE

"Victory or Death"

BY DECEMBER, 1776, the future of the thirteen United States looked grim indeed. When General Washington moved his ragged, outnumbered forces across the Delaware River into Pennsylvania to protect Philadelphia from attack, many influential citizens took sides with Britain. They believed the American cause was lost.

With the country's credit practically nonexistent, Congress struggled to meet the demands of the military, but Washington's troops were unpaid and all but destitute of supply. The commander in chief appealed to Robert Morris, merchant prince of Philadelphia, who raised funds that prevented the collapse of the Revolutionary effort at this crucial stage.

Morris was a wizard in money matters. Besides his own vast business and fleet of ships, he had influential friends and wide credit. He had to use this personal credit time and again to obtain funds for his country's needs. Once, when Morris was trying to raise on short notice a large sum that Washington required, he met a Quaker friend on the street, and then and there persuaded the man to advance him $50,000 on his word and bond.

Robert Morris lost about 150 of his own ships during

the war, most of them uninsured; but through some genius of management, he was always able to meet General Washington's urgent appeals.

While Committees of Safety gathered lead water spouts and clock and window weights to melt into bullets, men like Morris and Benjamin Franklin (whose delicate diplomacy won the aid of the French) were laying long-range plans for provisioning Washington's forces. So stupendous was their task that it took almost two years to supply American generals with enough weapons and ammunition to complete a major engagement.

European courts took care to prevent the export of arms and munitions to America. But Morris held rendezvous at night on the outskirts of Philadelphia with sympathetic contacts from foreign powers. His deals with these secret agents brought arms to the patriot troops.

It was funds Morris raised that enabled Washington and selected troops to recross the Delaware above Trenton on Christmas night. They startled and captured one thousand Hessians while Britain's General Howe celebrated the Yuletide in New York City.

Dr. Benjamin Rush visited General Washington at his quarters just before the crossing. The commander in chief kept scribbling on several small pieces of paper. One accidentally fell at Rush's feet. He couldn't help but wonder at the words he saw—"Victory or Death."

Rush discovered later that "in my interview with Genl. Washington, he had been meditating upon his attack upon the Hessians at their posts on the Jersey side of the Delaware, for I found that the countersign of his troops at the surprise of Trenton was 'Victory or Death.' "

It was victory this time for Washington. His successes at Trenton and Princeton made Philadelphians breathe easier, for they thought their city was saved from invasion. But the British sailed around to Chesapeake Bay and marched on the capital from the south. They defeated the Americans at the Battles of Brandywine and Germantown. On September 27, 1777, they took over Philadelphia and occupied it for the winter.

To escape capture, the Continental Congress fled to Baltimore, leaving Robert Morris to manage affairs at home.

Morris had come to America from Liverpool at thirteen to join his father, who was exporting tobacco from the colonies. He was orphaned at fifteen, and began to learn the shipping trade which made him wealthy. Out of his thirty years of sound business experience, Morris developed the qualities that made him the tireless, resourceful financier of the Revolution.

During the debate in Congress over separation from Britain, he had felt that the colonies were not ready to wage a successful war. However, he did not want to go on record against Independence; so he was one of the Pennsylvania delegates who stayed away from the State House the day Lee's resolution was put to vote. But he signed the Declaration.

In the month between the vote and the Signing, the Pennsylvania representation in Congress experienced a shake-up. Delegates opposing Independence withdrew. Elected to take their places were Dr. Rush, George Clymer, James Smith, George Taylor, and George Ross. All of them signed on August 2.

Clymer was a wealthy merchant. He was one of a committee left with Robert Morris in Philadelphia to conduct the business of Congress there. His home was in Chester County, directly in the path of the advancing enemy. After the Battle of Brandywine, the large Clymer family escaped to safer quarters. Their house was looted by British soldiers and all its furnishings destroyed.

Dr. Rush was one of the most distinguished of all the Signers. When his widowed mother started a grocery store to support her five children, there was little to suggest that her lively six-year-old Ben would become the most famous physician and professor of medicine in his time.

After earning his degree at the University of Edinburgh, he visited London and Benjamin Franklin, who was then abroad on diplomatic missions. Franklin gave Rush a letter of credit for £200 to finance a trip to Paris. "This kindness," said Rush, "attached me to him for the remainder of his life."

The gifted, versatile physician returned to Philadelphia to begin a phenomenal career. The political articles he wrote, favoring the cause of Independence, were widely read. It was he who suggested the title, *Common Sense*, to Thomas Paine for his famous booklet.

When Congress moved to Baltimore, and Philadelphians took measures for protection, Dr. Rush escorted his wife, Julie Stockton Rush, to Maryland, where the first of their thirteen children was born. He moved some of his furniture to the home of a friend in Darby, Pennsylvania. Later, during the occupation, British Commander Howe made his headquarters in that house on one of his excursions from Philadelphia. Dr. Rush related years later, ". . . on one of my mahogany tea tables he wrote his dispatches to England. . . . This table bears the marks of his ink to this day."

Dr. Rush joined the Philadelphia militia and cared for the wounded and dying. He barely escaped capture after the Battle of Brandywine.

Pennsylvania's Signer James Smith was a witty, well-educated Irishman who had begun his law practice in the western wilds. He later moved to York, Pennsylvania, and went into the iron business. Colonel Smith foresaw the break with Britain and trained militia long before war began. When Congress moved from Baltimore to York, the Board of War occupied his law office.

The colonel was full of funny stories, and his speeches in Congress were often highly entertaining. He could joke about almost anything—even the large fortune he lost and the two superintendents who helped him lose it through mismanagement of his business while he was absent on patriotic duties. But there were two things about which he never joked—religion and George Washington, whom he greatly admired.

In the spring of 1777, General Washington and financier Morris, two of the busiest men of the time, appeared at the little upholstery shop of John and Betsy Ross on Arch Street in Philadelphia, near the State House. Accompanying them was John's uncle, George Ross. The three had brought a design for an American flag which they wanted Betsy to make. This design indicated six-pointed stars on a blue square in the upper left-hand corner of a field of red and white stripes. Betsy suggested that five-pointed stars be used.

With a fine stitch, she proceeded to make the first Star-Spangled Banner, with thirteen stars and thirteen stripes to honor the colonies that had agreed to the Declaration of Independence. On June 14, Congress approved this design.

Jolly Uncle George Ross was a prominent lawyer of Lancaster, Pennsylvania, who had served in the First Continental Congress. He was not re-elected to the Second Congress until the change in delegates in July of '76.

Ross had a sister Gertrude who was married to Delaware Signer George Read, vice-president of his state. Gertrude was in Philadelphia with her husband and family when he was summoned home to succeed the president (governor), who had been taken prisoner by the enemy. To avoid capture themselves, the Reads proceeded cautiously along the Jersey shore of the Delaware River.

An armed barge from the British men-of-war pursued them as they crossed the river. The tide was out. Their boat went aground. Quickly, they removed all identifying marks from their luggage. As the British officers came alongside, Read assumed the role of a country gentleman returning home with his family. Whereupon, the British sailors good-naturedly helped carry Signer Read's mother, Gertrude, and the small children to shore!

While many of the Signers were born to wealth and fine educational advantages, there were those whose early days were difficult and humble. In fact, George Taylor began his life in America as a bond servant! He gave up studying medicine in Ireland and, without even a sixpence in his pocket, boarded a vessel bound for America as a redemptioner. A man who owned an iron works in Pennsylvania's Bucks County paid his expenses.

Young George was set to feeding coal to the blast furnaces. He developed such blisters that his employer, perceiving the boy's intelligence, suggested that he might handle a pen better than a shovel. So he became a clerk, though a bond servant still.

Apparently George made out well at the iron works.

Some years later, at any rate, he married the widow of the man who had paid his passage to America.

Taylor expanded the industry and acquired a considerable fortune. He served in the Provincial Assembly and consistently opposed British imperialism. His neighbors called him a "fine and furious Whig." His period in Congress was brief. But he served his country diligently in deals with the Indians and suffered financial losses because he was away so much.

Also an immigrant was the stern, nearsighted Scot, James Wilson, who had come to America ten years before the Signing. He had studied at the Universities of St. Andrews, Glasgow, and Edinburgh.

Wilson was a bold, decided man with a powerful voice who became one of the eminent lawyers of Pennsylvania. Dr. Rush said of him, "Not a word ever fell from his lips out of time, or out of place, nor could a word be taken from or added to his speeches without injuring them." He was among the first to declare that Parliament had no authority to rule over the colonies.

Signer John Morton was born near Philadelphia in humble circumstances. John's stepfather taught him his own profession of surveying and gave him a good education. He began his public life as justice of the peace and rose to associate judge of the Supreme Court of Pennsylvania.

For a long time he was a Loyalist, like the others of

his locality. But his political opinions changed as Britain's tyranny continued, and he cast his vote for Independence. His neighbors and friends, even many of his relatives, then turned upon him. He was a sensitive man, and those who knew him were convinced that this social ostracism hastened his death in April, 1777, eight months after he affixed his signature to the Declaration.

John Morton was the first of all the Signers to die. His last words were, ". . . tell them that they will live to see the hour when they shall acknowledge it to have been the most glorious service that I ever rendered to my country."

CHAPTER

They Signed for Us

WILLIAM WHIPPLE
New Hampshire

JOSIAH BARTLETT
New Hampshire

MATTHEW THORNTON
New Hampshire

ROGER SHERMAN
Connecticut

SAMUEL HUNTINGTON
Connecticut

WILLIAM WILLIAMS
Connecticut

SIX

"Turn Out and Crush Burgoyne"

THE DELEGATES in Congress put in exhausting days and nights prosecuting the war. They were family men, most of them away from their homes and chosen vocations for months at a time. Important committee sessions often were held of an evening in the pleasant informality of a coffeehouse or inn. With business disposed of, the weary delegates would relax with good talk and refreshment. Often it was venerable Stephen Hopkins of Rhode Island who, as John Adams put it, "kept us all alive."

This witty Quaker entertained until midnight with his anecdotes, dissertations on history, and gems from Milton and Pope. Sharing these sessions with Hopkins as a fellow member of the Naval Committee, Adams recalled his memories of them as the most delightful of all his years in Congress.

Stephen Hopkins, nine times governor of Rhode Island, had little formal education. He read and studied by himself sufficiently to become a distinguished mathematician, a representative in the Provincial Assembly, chief justice of the colony, and the first chancellor of

Rhode Island College (later Brown University). Called the country's first abolitionist, he made strong efforts for legislation to free slaves in his colony and granted freedom to every slave he owned.

In full agreement with him on the slavery question was his fellow Signer from Rhode Island, William Ellery, who worked hard to abolish slavery in the United States. Ellery was a lawyer and Harvard graduate. The British felt particular hostility toward him because of his active and outspoken patriotism. When he signed the Declaration, he pledged a large fortune, which he lost within a few months to the cause.

On the very day in December, 1776, that Washington crossed the Delaware, the British captured Ellery's home town of Newport, Rhode Island, and occupied it for three years. He left Congress for a few weeks to participate in a scheme to drive the British from Newport, but the effort failed. Through Congress, he did manage to relieve the distress of victims of the invasion. The British burned Ellery's house and destroyed almost all of his property.

In the summer of 1777, the British began their campaign to separate New England from the other colonies. But British plans went awry. Their General Burgoyne became isolated in the northern Hudson Valley. General Washington called on "all New England to turn out and crush Burgoyne." New England forces closed in, and the Indians assisting Burgoyne deserted him. The American victory at Saratoga, one of the great decisive battles of history, forced Burgoyne to surrender on October 17, 1777.

Signer William Whipple, a brigadier general in command of New Hampshire troops, was one of the commissioners who, on behalf of General Gates, arranged and signed the terms of Burgoyne's capitulation. He was one of the officers chosen to guard the prisoners of war on the march to Winter Hill, near Boston.

General Whipple was a cool commander, a prosperous Portsmouth merchant, and an able seaman, all of which made him an extremely valuable member of Congress during these hazardous times. He had gone to sea as a cabin boy, which was considered necessary training for a successful merchant's career. He worked his way up and retired from the sea as a captain at twenty-nine.

He commanded a detachment of New Hampshire troops on an expedition to Rhode Island. One morning, while having breakfast with his officers, General Whipple narrowly escaped serious injury. A British cannon ball whizzed under the table, struck a brigade major, and shattered his leg so badly that it had to be amputated.

All three of the New Hampshire delegates were military men, two of whom were doctors. Colonel Josiah Bartlett's brilliant talents, quick mind, and tenacious memory made him a leading patriot in the poor frontier colony of New Hampshire. Bribes had been offered him by the royal governor, but the physician refused them and continued to work for Independence. Consequently, the governor dismissed him as justice of the peace and deprived him of his military commission.

When Dr. Bartlett was elected to the First Continental Congress, he could not attend because his house had been burned, presumably because of his patriotic views. He was elected to the Second Continental Congress and had the honor, together with his colleague William Whipple, of being the first to vote for Independence. It is thought that Josiah Bartlett was the first, following President Hancock, to sign the Declaration. Delegates signed by colonies, starting with the most northern. Dr. Bartlett signed, as was the custom of the day, at the extreme right.

Dr. Matthew Thornton, of New Hampshire, a sober-faced Irishman full of funny stories, appeared in Congress three months after the Signing. He added his name at the lower right below the signatures of the Connecticut delegates.

Two of the four Connecticut Signers struggled hard for their early education. Roger Sherman was apprenticed to a shoemaker and gained his elementary schooling largely from reading books propped up on his shoemaker's bench. When he became a partner of his merchant brother, he had time to study law. Shrewd and able, Sherman became a leading patriot in Connecticut and rose rapidly in public office. He was chosen treasurer of Yale College and received an honorary degree of Master of Arts. He attended the First and the Second Continental Congress and served on the committee to draft the Declaration.

Like his colleague, Roger Sherman, Samuel Huntington had a meager education, but he taught himself from borrowed books. His father was a farmer, and young Samuel, a fourth-generation American, was apprenticed to a cooper. He studied law by himself and established a good practice. He became associate judge of the Superior Court of Connecticut. Huntington was an economical, modest, thoughtful man who talked little. He rose from plowboy to what was then called president of Congress.

William Williams, the son-in-law of the governor of Connecticut, replaced General Oliver Wolcott in Congress. Williams, a Harvard graduate, gave up theology to become a merchant in Lebanon, Connecticut, but he closed his business when the Revolution broke out. He was generous in helping to meet military needs. His house was always open to American soldiers. When the French allies wintered in Lebanon, he moved his family out of his own home so the French officers might have more comfortable winter quarters.

They Signed for Us

Edward Rutledge J.	**EDWARD RUTLEDGE** *South Carolina*
Arthur Middleton	**ARTHUR MIDDLETON** *South Carolina*
Thos Heyward Junr.	**THOMAS HEYWARD, JR.** *South Carolina*
Thomas Lynch Junr	**THOMAS LYNCH, JR.** *South Carolina*
Lyman Hall	**LYMAN HALL** *Georgia*
Geo Walton.	**GEORGE WALTON** *Georgia*

SEVEN

"The World Turned Upside Down"

BUTTON GWINNETT
Georgia

JOHN PENN
North Carolina

WILLIAM HOOPER
North Carolina

JOSEPH HEWES
North Carolina

THOMAS NELSON, JR.
Virginia

CARTER BRAXTON
Virginia

PATRIOTISM in South Carolina had a provincial emphasis. The colony did not think of itself as separating from the mother country. Its leaders were absorbed, that spring of 1776, in setting up a new colonial government and adopting a constitution. The mature in judgment were needed at home; the younger men were more easily spared to look after the business in the Continental Congress.

Consequently, the South Carolina delegation was the youngest at the time of the Signing. The average age of the four plantation aristocrats who affixed their names to the Declaration was just twenty-nine years. The youngest, Edward Rutledge, became a member of the First Continental Congress before he was twenty-five. At twenty-six, he distinguished himself as the youngest Signer of them all. Rutledge's colleagues were his brother-in-law, Arthur Middleton; Thomas Heyward, Jr.; and Thomas Lynch, Jr. The four had more than age, wealth, and family background in common. All had studied law at the Middle Temple in London. Each, upon returning to America, had entered public life.

Arthur Middleton, who was thirty-four in 1776 and the eldest of the quartet, came from an immensely wealthy family. His father owned several plantations and about eight hundred slaves.

Young Middleton did not get up to Philadelphia until

a few weeks before Lee's resolution came to a vote. Thomas Heyward went about the same time. He was an amiable fellow and was considered quite a poet. Thomas Lynch, who lost out to Rutledge as the youngest Signer by just three months, had been dispatched to Philadelphia to care for and, as it turned out, to substitute for his delegate father, who had suffered a stroke. His own health was precarious.

The four young men all saw military service. In 1775, Lynch was appointed to command a company. On a march to British-threatened Charleston, he became violently ill. Privation and exposure aggravated a condition from which he never fully recovered. His health declined alarmingly while he was in Congress, and signing the Declaration was one of his last political acts. A change of climate was the only hope physicians could suggest. He and his young wife sailed for the south of France. Presumably, their ship foundered in a violent storm, which was reported by another vessel. The Lynches were never heard of again.

When Middleton, Rutledge, and Heyward returned from Philadelphia, they served as officers in the militia. All three were captured during the forty-day siege of Charleston and were taken to St. Augustine on a prison ship. There, for ten months, they suffered privations and indignities until the formal exchange of prisoners at the end of the war. The magnificent estates of Middleton and Rutledge were devastated.

By 1779, the British were confident that the North was all but won. They had wrought frightful damage to military installations. They held or had disabled so many ports that patriot shipping was paralyzed. General Washington warned Congress that he might have to stop fighting for a year until his forces could recover.

The theater of war had moved to the South, which was even more torn by violence between Whigs and Tories than was the North. This was an ugly, vicious, hateful period, in which even women, children, and slaves were forced into woods and swamps to die.

By late 1779, the enemy had forced the sparsely settled coastal strip called Georgia into submission. There was strong Loyalist sentiment there, but the state's three delegates to Congress all had favored Independence. Lyman Hall, Button Gwinnett, and George Walton made a strong, united stand against foreign domination.

When the British captured Savannah, Colonel Walton, badly wounded, was taken prisoner. The enemy destroyed the home of Dr. Hall and confiscated his rice plantation.

Button Gwinnett, an Englishman who had come to Savannah in 1765, was commissioned president of Georgia and commander in chief of its military forces after Independence was declared. But, in May, 1777, he was so badly wounded in a duel with a political adversary that he died a few days later. He was the second Signer to die.

Two of North Carolina's three representatives in Congress in '76, John Penn and William Hooper, were lawyers, and the third, Joseph Hewes, was a prosperous merchant. A knowledge of shipping made Hewes a valuable member of the Marine Committee in Congress. He knew the Revolutionary hero, John Paul Jones, and was instrumental in procuring a ship for him. Hewes died during his term of service in Philadelphia, presumably from overwork. Hooper and his family were endangered by the British and driven from their home near Wilmington, North Carolina.

The Signer who wrote "Thos. Nelson, jr.," on the famous parchment was a grandson of "Scotch Tom" Nelson, who founded one of the richest families in Virginia. The "jr." was to distinguish him from an uncle of the same name. The Nelsons, prominent merchants and planters, lived at Yorktown. Thomas, the Signer, was associated in business with a tobacco man named Reynolds.

He became a member of the Virginia Council at twenty-six. At the meeting in St. John's Church, Richmond, in March, 1775, Nelson asked for the floor a few minutes before Patrick Henry delivered his famous speech.

The chair recognized him: "The gentleman from York County."

"I am a merchant of Yorktown," Thomas Nelson said, "but I am a Virginian first. Let my trade perish. I call

God to witness that if any British troops are landed in the County of York, of which I am lieutenant, I will wait for no orders, but will summon the militia and drive the invaders into the sea."

Several of his colleagues jumped to their feet at this brash declaration.

It was Nelson who bore to Philadelphia the following year, in May, the resolution of the Virginia Convention which Lee presented to Congress. A year after he placed his signature on the Declaration, Nelson left Congress for military service. He commanded the Virginia militia as brigadier general. At the age of forty-two, he became third governor of his state, succeeding Thomas Jefferson.

Late in 1780, the fortunes of war began to turn in favor of the Americans. Frontiersmen defeated detachments of the British army in encounters in the Carolinas. Washington saw that the need now was aid for the inadequate southern forces opposing the British general, Charles, Earl Cornwallis.

By August, 1781, Cornwallis had moved his army toward Chesapeake Bay and was holding a position at Yorktown. The village was bounded on three sides by water; Cornwallis counted on British naval strength to protect him and guarantee his supply.

Most of the American troops were in New York with Washington, who determined to co-ordinate all possible sea and land forces, both French and American, in one giant effort against Cornwallis. The story of this accomplishment became an epic in the military and naval history of the world.

The twenty-three-year-old French leader, Marquis de Lafayette, marched his troops from Richmond toward Yorktown. In the north, Washington and the French general, Rochambeau, walked their troops all the way to Chesapeake Bay because there were no ships to transport them. Naval reinforcements from France by way of Haiti, under the command of Comte de Grasse, beat the British fleet to the Chesapeake. De Grasse then sent ships to Annapolis to meet the American and French troops. Cornwallis was closed in at Yorktown like a ship in a bottle.

On September 18, Washington, Lafayette, and Governor Nelson, with their aides, accepted De Grasse's invitation to board his flagship. There details for the siege of Yorktown were worked out.

Residents of the village had fled to safety behind the patriot lines. One man who chose to remain with his property was the governor's uncle, Thomas Nelson, Sr. Cornwallis had commandeered the uncle's fine house for headquarters.

On September 28, the American and French land forces, 16,000 in number, took their positions in a semicircle about the town. By October 9, they had dug in and were ready. At three o'clock in the afternoon they opened bombardment with seventy cannon.

The siege lasted three weeks. The British soon retreated to rear positions within Yorktown. Homes and business houses were riddled. In scenes of horror, rich furnishings and books were strewn in the same earth with the mangled bodies of horses and men.

Allied bombardment so reduced the elder Nelson's home that Cornwallis was forced to seek quarters elsewhere. At this point, the uncle asked permission of the British general to pass through the lines to the patriot side and his own family. Cornwallis consented, and Thomas Nelson, Sr., crossed under a "flag of truce." As quickly as he could, he made his way to the side of the governor, who was commander in chief of the Virginia militia. The uncle said he thought Cornwallis and his staff were moving to the governor's home.

Later, on a tour of inspection, Governor Nelson watched his men fire on his own neighborhood. "Why do you spare my house?" he demanded of a gunner.

"Out of respect to you, sir," the soldier replied.

"Give me the cannon!" Nelson ordered. He directed the fire upon his own stately dwelling.

At ten o'clock on the morning of October 17, a drummer in red, accompanied by an officer with a flag of truce, appeared on a British parapet on the south side of Yorktown to beat a "parley." Cornwallis was asking for surrender terms!

On the afternoon of the nineteenth, the British army, clad in a new issue of uniforms, marched out from Yorktown with fife and drum playing an old British air, "The World Turned Upside Down." The sword of surrender was presented by one of the generals under Cornwallis, who pleaded illness as his reason for absence from the field of defeat. Then, between a mile-long column of American and French troops, the British marched to a designated spot to stack their muskets and lay down all arms.

The Revolutionary War was virtually at an end. The United States of America was a free and independent nation!

The cost of war had no ending. Governor Nelson had raised a necessary $2,000,000 almost overnight by putting up his own properties as collateral. They were forfeited when the loans came due. His government never reimbursed him. With health as well as fortune ruined, Thomas Nelson, Jr., removed with his large family to a modest place in a neighboring county. He died of asthma eight years later, a little over fifty years of age.

Sharing in the price of victory was his fellow Virginian, Signer Carter Braxton, whose fortune was invested in ships. Braxton's vessels were seized by the enemy or otherwise lost. Many of his debtors were unable to pay him, and he spent the rest of his life in dire financial straits.

THE FIFTY-SIX men who affixed their signatures to the Declaration of Independence were, for the most part, a young, vigorous, and hardy lot. Only seven were over sixty; eighteen were still in their thirties; and three in their twenties. Not one wore a beard or mustache.

Considering the average life span of their time, most of these patriots lived to a remarkable age. Three lived to be over ninety. Ten died in their eighties. If George Wythe had not been poisoned by a grandnephew impatient for his inheritance, the distinguished old scholar would have exceeded his eighty years.

Maryland's Charles Carroll outlived by six years the last of the other Signers. On the Fourth of July, 1828, he spaded the first earth for the Baltimore and Ohio Railroad, which would unite the East with the West. Carroll died in 1832, at the age of ninety-five.

Only two of the Signers were bachelors. Sixteen married twice. Records indicate that at least two, and possibly as many as six, were childless. But the remaining Signers fathered close to 325 children! Carter Braxton of Virginia compensated for several small families by having eighteen. William Ellery of Rhode Island had

EIGHT

of Worthies"

seventeen children; Roger Sherman of Connecticut had fifteen.

The Signers were men devoted to their belief in a Creator who had fashioned them in His image and likeness. That meant, they stoutly contended, that they were to be free rather than enslaved. Since the Church of England prevailed in the colonies, considerably more than half of the fifty-six expressed their religious faith in Episcopalian worship. Charles Carroll was Roman Catholic; the others were Congregational, Presbyterian, Quaker, or Baptist. Ten Signers were preachers' sons.

Only a few Signers fell into obscurity after the significant days of '76. Most of them served state and nation with honor for many years. John Adams became the first vice-president of the United States and its second president. Thomas Jefferson served under him as vice-president, then succeeded him to the presidency. Elbridge Gerry, who once had fled the redcoats in his nightshirt, had ample opportunity to display a proper dignity thereafter. He was vice-president under James Madison. Gerry died in his carriage in his seventy-first year while on his way to preside over the Senate.

Fifty years after the Signing, in 1826, only Charles

Carroll and those two stalwarts, John Adams and Thomas Jefferson, remained alive.

Through their long years of friendship, Adams and Jefferson had disagreed on many basic issues. Around the turn of the century, political differences estranged them. They were reconciled partly through the efforts of a self-appointed mediator, Dr. Benjamin Rush. Most of the credit unquestionably was due to their own wisdom in recognizing that neither men nor nations need forgo friendship because they do not agree at every point. The two spent many long hours of their declining years—one at his beloved Monticello near Charlottesville, Virginia, the other in Quincy, Massachusetts—writing philosophical letters to each other.

Jefferson had pledged himself, when he first took public office, never to misuse his trust to promote his personal fortunes. His forty years of service to his country often deprived him of time and energy for his own business affairs. Although he had inherited a considerable estate, and had enhanced that by marrying a wealthy young widow, the author of the Declaration of Independence spent his last years staving off bankruptcy.

The chief trial of Adams' old age was the loss of his beloved wife, Abigail, who died thirteen years before he did. Death also claimed three children. His eldest son, John Quincy, became the sixth president of the United States.

As the Fourth of July, 1826, drew near, festivities marking fifty years of freedom were planned the length and breadth of the U.S.A. The three living Signers were invited to be present at a significant gathering in Washington, D.C. But old John Adams, now almost ninety-one, was too feeble even to participate in the celebration at Quincy. At Monticello, Thomas Jefferson, eight years younger, lay on his deathbed.

In a dramatic climax that even their agile minds would not have contemplated, these two principals in the struggle for Independence left the nation awe-stricken and touched by dying hours apart on the Fourth of July. Jefferson died at one o'clock in the afternoon, Adams toward evening.

Jefferson had written his last letter on June 24, addressed to the mayor of Washington, who had issued the invitation:

"I should, indeed, with peculiar delight, have met ... with the small band, the remnant of that host of worthies, who joined with us on that day, in the bold and doubtful election we were to make for our country, between submission or the sword; and to have enjoyed with them the consolatory fact, that our fellow-citizens, after half a century of experience and prosperity, continue to approve the choice we made.... All eyes are opened to the rights of man ... let the annual return of this day forever refresh our recollection of these rights, and an undiminished devotion to them."

Bibliography

AUGUR, HELEN. *The Secret War of Independence*. New York: Duell, Sloan & Pearce, 1955.

CHINARD, GILBERT. *Honest John Adams*. Boston: Little, Brown, 1933.

GOODRICH, CHARLES. *Lives of the Signers of the Declaration of Independence*. New York: Reed & Company, 1829.

IRVING, WASHINGTON. *Life of George Washington*. 5 vols. New York: G. P. Putnam & Co., 1857-59.

LOSSING, BENSON J. *Pictorial Field-Book of the Revolution*. New York: Harper Brothers, 1850.

————. *Signers of the Declaration of Independence*. New York: George F. Cooledge & Brother, 1848.

MALONE, DUMAS; MILHOLLEN, HIRST; and KAPLAN, MILTON. *The Story of the Declaration of Independence*. New York: Oxford University Press, 1954.

McGEE, DOROTHY HORTON. *Famous Signers of the Declaration*. New York: Dodd, Mead & Company, 1956.

PADOVER, SAUL K. *A Jefferson Profile*. New York: The John Day Company, 1956.

SANDERSON, JOHN, and WALN, ROBERT, JR. *Biography of the Signers to the Declaration of Independence*. 9 vols. Philadelphia: R. W. Pomeroy, 1823-27.

THOMPSON, CHARLES O. F. *A History of the Declaration of Independence*. Bristol, Rhode Island: Published by the author, 1947.

Signers of the Declaration of Independence

New Hampshire

    Josiah Bartlett, 1729-1795
    Matthew Thornton, 1714(?)-1803
    William Whipple, 1730-1785

Massachusetts

    John Adams, 1735-1826
    Samuel Adams, 1722-1803
    Elbridge Gerry, 1744-1814
    John Hancock, 1737-1793
    Robert Treat Paine, 1731-1814

Rhode Island

    William Ellery, 1727-1820
    Stephen Hopkins, 1707-1785

Connecticut

    Samuel Huntington, 1731-1796
    Roger Sherman, 1721-1793
    William Williams, 1731-1811
    Oliver Wolcott, 1726-1797

New York

> William Floyd, 1734-1821
> Francis Lewis, 1713-1803
> Philip Livingston, 1716-1778
> Lewis Morris, 1726-1798

New Jersey

> Abraham Clark, 1726-1794
> John Hart, 1711(?)-1779
> Francis Hopkinson, 1737-1791
> Richard Stockton, 1730-1781
> John Witherspoon, 1723-1794

Maryland

> Charles Carroll, 1737-1832
> Samuel Chase, 1741-1811
> William Paca, 1740-1799
> Thomas Stone, 1743-1787

Delaware

> Thomas McKean, 1734-1817
> George Read, 1733-1798
> Caesar Rodney, 1728-1784

Pennsylvania

> George Clymer, 1739-1813
> Benjamin Franklin, 1706-1790
> Robert Morris, 1734-1806
> John Morton, 1724(?)-1777
> George Ross, 1730-1779

Pennsylvania—Continued

Benjamin Rush, 1745(?)-1813
James Smith, 1719(?)-1806
George Taylor, 1716-1781
James Wilson, 1742-1798

Virginia

Carter Braxton, 1736-1797
Benjamin Harrison, 1726(?)-1791
Thomas Jefferson, 1743-1826
Francis Lightfoot Lee, 1734-1797
Richard Henry Lee, 1732-1794
Thomas Nelson, Jr., 1738-1789
George Wythe, 1726-1806

North Carolina

Joseph Hewes, 1730-1779
William Hooper, 1742-1790
John Penn, 1741(?)-1788

South Carolina

Thomas Heyward, Jr., 1746-1809
Thomas Lynch, Jr., 1749-1779
Arthur Middleton, 1742-1787
Edward Rutledge, 1749-1800

Georgia

Button Gwinnett, 1735(?)-1777
Lyman Hall, 1724(?)-1790
George Walton, 1741(?)-1804

Index

the ten commandments

CHARLES L. ALLEN is pastor of the First Methodist Church of Houston, Texas, one of the nation's largest Protestant congregations. Known widely through speaking engagements, through radio and television appearances, and as a newspaper columnist, he is the author of a number of inspirational books, which have enjoyed sales of over 1,000,000 copies. Among these are *God's Psychiatry*, of which *The Ten Commandments* was originally a part, *All Things Are Possible Through Prayer*, *Healing Words*, *Twelve Ways to Solve Your Problem* and *Prayer Changes Things*.

Books by CHARLES L. ALLEN

ALL THINGS ARE POSSIBLE THROUGH PRAYER

GOD'S PSYCHIATRY

HEALING WORDS

IN QUEST OF GOD'S POWER

THE LIFE OF CHRIST

THE LORD'S PRAYER

PRAYER CHANGES THINGS

ROADS TO RADIANT LIVING

THE TOUCH OF THE MASTER'S HAND

TWELVE WAYS TO SOLVE YOUR PROBLEM

THE TWENTY-THIRD PSALM

WHEN THE HEART IS HUNGRY

WHEN YOU LOSE A LOVED ONE

THE TEN
COMMANDMENTS
An Interpretation

CHARLES L. ALLEN

FLEMING H. REVELL COMPANY

Illustrations by Ismar David

I

THOU SHALT HAVE NO OTHER GODS BEFORE ME

SHORTLY AFTER MOSES LED THE CHILDREN OF Israel away from the bondage of Egypt on their journey to the promised land, God called Moses up on Mt. Sinai. He must have said something like this: "Moses, your people are now headed toward prosperity. The land I have promised to them is rich and productive and will supply not only their needs, but much more. In fact, the land flows with milk and honey. But, Moses, people cannot be made happy and successful merely by the possession of things. The way they live is more important than what they have. So, I am going to give you ten rules for living. I want you to teach the people these rules. If they live by them, I promise they will be blessed. But I warn you, if they break these rules they will be severely penalized. And one other thing, Moses —these are to be the rules of living for all peoples of all times. They will never go out of date; they will never be repealed or changed."

We have those rules, known as the Ten Commandments, recorded in Exodus 20. They are not only the basis of conduct, both moral and spiritual, but also the basis of peace and prosperity for the individual and for the world. The Bible says, "The fool hath said in his heart, There is no God" (PSALM 14:1), and it is only a fool who thinks he is big enough or smart enough to violate the unchangeable laws of the eternal God and

6

get by with it. No man can break God's law; he breaks only himself.

Very important is the order in which God stated His laws. The first four deal with man's relationship with God, the last six with man's relationship with man. Before man can live rightly with other men, he must first get right with God. Someone has said, "The golden rule is my religion," but the golden rule is nobody's religion, because it is not a religion. It is merely the expression of religion.

As H. G. Wells put it, "Until a man has found God he begins at no beginning; he works to no end."

The first commandment is somewhat surprising. We would think that it would be, "Thou shalt believe in a God," a law against atheism. There is no such law. God took care of that in our creation. We do not teach a baby to hunger or to thirst; nature does that. However, we must train our children to satisfy their hungers and thirsts with the right things.

Man instinctively believes and worships. Nowhere does the Bible attempt to prove the existence of God. Man is created incomplete, and he cannot be at rest until there is a satisfaction of his deepest hunger, the yearning of his soul. The danger lies in that fact that man can pervert his worship instinct and make for himself a false god.

St. Augustine said, "My soul is restless until it finds it can rest in Thee, O God." No false god satisfies the longing of the soul, but we can, and many do,

squander our lives seeking satisfaction from false objects of worship. So the first of God's rules for life is: "Thou shalt have no other gods before me."

At Vicksburg, Mississippi, an engineer showed me an almost dry channel. He explained that once the great Mississippi river flowed there, but now it had been changed into another channel which had been dug. The flow of the river could not be stopped, but it could be diverted. So with our worship of God. Man is incomplete without an object of worship; the yearning of his soul demands attention. But man can turn from the one true God and make for himself another god. There have been people who worshiped the sun, or a star, or a mountain. In some countries people worship a cow, or a river, or something else. We think of those people as being primitive. They are, but no more primitive than multitudes of people in this enlightened land we call America. God said, "Thou shalt have no other gods before me," and that law of life we are guilty of breaking.

There are five objects of worship which multitudes today have put before God: wealth, fame, pleasure, power, and knowledge. While most of us have no idea of ever being really rich, we never become satisfied with what we can reasonably possess. Maybe that is good, except when that dissatisfaction obscures our feelings for God and diverts us in our search for God. I can become so interested in what I have that I forget the needs of my soul.

Most of us never expect to be famous, yet the little child says, "See how high I can jump, or watch me run." We are born with the desire to be noticed. That is not wrong. God made us separate identities, and we do want to be known. Yet, as a minister, I counsel with many people who have wrecked their lives and destroyed their happiness simply because they have not received the attention they desired. Many get their feelings hurt at the smallest slight. We in America spend more money on cosmetics, for example, than we spend on the entire program of the Kingdom of God. It isn't wrong to want to look our best. But it is wrong when putting ourselves forward becomes our first desire, thus our god.

All men want to be happy, but we make a mistake when we think pleasure is the way to get happiness. There is forgetfulness of life's routines in pleasures, but they do not satisfy the soul. Pleasure is like dope; gradually we must increase the dose with more excitement, more thrill, more sensation, until, eventually, we find ourselves groping among the tombstones of our dead passions. It is like making our meals out of pickles and pepper. One of our greatest temptations is to put pleasure before God.

Power is not wrong, neither is knowledge. The electric power in America is the equal of one hundred and fifty slaves for each of us and is a great blessing to us. But power worshiped turns us into little Hitlers. Knowledge is good, but the worship of knowledge

9

destroys obedience, just as the worship of power destroys character.

To worship God leads us to be like God and to obey His will. Thus we become good and walk in the paths of right living when we have no other gods before God.

II
THOU SHALT NOT MAKE UNTO THEE ANY GRAVEN IMAGE

THOU SHALT NOT MAKE UNTO THEE ANY GRAVEN
IMAGE, OR ANY LIKENESS OF ANY THING THAT IS IN
HEAVEN ABOVE, OR THAT IS IN THE EARTH
BENEATH, OR THAT IS IN THE WATER UNDER THE
EARTH. THOU SHALT NOT BOW DOWN THYSELF TO
THEM, NOR SERVE THEM: FOR I THE LORD THY GOD
AM A JEALOUS GOD, VISITING THE INIQUITY OF
THE FATHERS UPON THE CHILDREN UNTO THE
THIRD AND FOURTH GENERATION OF THEM THAT
HATE ME; AND SHEWING MERCY UNTO THOUSANDS
OF THEM THAT LOVE ME, AND KEEP MY
COMMANDMENTS

THE SECOND RULE OF GOD IS, "THOU SHALT NOT
make unto thee any graven image." This is the one rule
that most people feel less guilty of breaking, yet more is
said about this one in the Bible than any other. Primitive man found it hard to realize a God he could not
see, so he made aids to assist his imagination, to bring
reality into his worship. That is not wrong. Frank
Boreham tells of a man who prayed with a vacant chair
before him. He imagined God sitting in that chair, and
it made his prayers more real.

On my desk are several copies of the Bible. I use
them in my studying and devotional reading, yet they
would be of value to me, even if I never opened them.
Their very presence serves to remind me of God. Of
course, one can worship anywhere, but worship is

easier in the church building. Not only the building, but the ritual, the music and the sermon also are aids to worship.

The danger lies in the fact that it is so easy to worship the means instead of the goal. The Bible, churches, music, and ministers, and all our symbols and aids to worship are sacred only because they lead us to God. For example, denominationalism can be a violation of this rule. I am a Methodist, but I could be just as good a Christian if I were a Baptist or a Presbyterian or a member of any denomination which says with Peter, "Thou art the Christ, the Son of the living God" (MATTHEW 16:16).

Even more dangerous than our aids to worship are some other images we make. We are told that "God created man in his own image" (GENESIS 1:27). But to live a life in conformity with our creation is difficult. In fact, it is so difficult that all of us fall far short. Thus, instead of being like God, we seek to create Him in our own image. It is so much easier to make God like ourselves than for us to be like Him.

God tells us not to do wrong, but there are some things we want to do, right or wrong. So we create a God who doesn't care what we do. We think of the God of the blue skies, majestic mountains and lovely flowers, but turn our backs on the God who said, ". . . ye have robbed me . . . In tithes and offerings" (MALACHI 3:8), or the God who said, ". . . whatsoever a man soweth, that shall he also reap" (GALATIANS

13

6:7). It has been well pointed out that Christ was not crucified because He said, "Consider the lilies, how they grow," but rather because He said, "Consider the thieves, how they steal."

It is so much easier to whittle God down to our size instead of repenting, changing our way of living, and being Godly ourselves. When Horace Bushnell was a college student he felt he was an atheist. One day a voice seemed to say to him, "If you do not believe in God, what do you believe?" He answered back, "I believe there is a difference between right and wrong." "Are you living up to the highest you believe?" the voice seemed to ask. "No," he said, "but I will." That day he dedicated his life to his highest belief. Years later, after he had been pastor of one church forty-seven years, he said, "Better than I know any person in my church, I know Jesus Christ." When he began conforming his life to his beliefs, instead of making his beliefs fit his life, he was led to a realization of God.

The very process of thinking requires mental pictures or images. Think of an apple, and you see one in your imagination. Think of Abraham Lincoln, and his face is flashed on the screen of your mind. And when one thinks of God, he sees some picture of God. The danger lies in the fact that it can be the wrong picture, which can be tragic. One becomes like his image of God, and if it is the wrong image the man becomes wrong. So the Bible contains more warning in

14

regard to God's second rule for life, "Thou shalt not make unto thee any graven image" (EXODUS 20:4), than in regard to any of the other ten.

Man sees a little of God in many forms—majesty in His mountains, greatness in His seas, loveliness in His flowers, righteousness in His saints. But all of these are insufficient. With Philip, the heart of each of us says, "Lord, show us the Father," Jesus replied, "He that hath seen me hath seen the Father" (JOHN 14:8,9). The only perfect image of God we have is Christ, and that is sufficient.

As you see Him through the words of the Gospels—Matthew, Mark, Luke, and John—you are impressed with His eyes. Those who were with Him in the flesh neglected to tell us much about His physical appearance, but they could not forget His eyes. "And the Lord turned, and looked upon Peter" (LUKE 22:61), and Peter broke down. Sometimes Jesus' eyes flashed with merriment, sometimes they melted in tenderness, and other times they were filled with stern rebuke. When I read, "The ways of man are before the eyes of the Lord" (PROVERBS 5:21), I stop still in my tracks and think on my ways.

When we look at Jesus' face we know it was a happy face. Little children ran to get in His lap and clasp Him around His neck. People invited Him to their parties. Seeing God in Christ, we are not afraid of Him; instead we want to be closer to Him. We listen as He says, "Neither do I condemn thee: go, and sin

15

no more" (JOHN 8:11), and we are ashamed of our sins, we want forgiveness, and we come to Him repenting and asking for His cleansing.

We look as "he stedfastly set his face to go to Jerusalem" (LUKE 9:51). Though it meant death, He would not go back on the high purposes of His life. Seeing Him puts the steel in our own backbones to make the right decision. We watch as He walked seven miles to Emmaus to give hope to the downhearted (LUKE 24:13-32), or as He gave a new chance to His friends who failed Him (JOHN 20:19-31), and we take new heart and new hope.

How wonderful it is to see God. To encourage the early Christians who were bearing almost the unbearable, John says to them that those who are faithful "shall see his face" (REVELATION 22:4). The promise of seeing Him compensated for any sacrifice.

One thing more. After Thorwaldsen had completed his famous statue of Christ, he brought a friend to see it. Christ's arms were outstretched, His head bowed between them. The friend said, "But I cannot see His face." The sculptor replied, "If you would see the face of Christ, you must get on your knees." He is the perfect image of God; let us have no other.

III

THOU SHALT NOT TAKE THE NAME OF THE LORD THY GOD IN VAIN

GOD'S THIRD RULE FOR LIVING IS, "THOU SHALT not take the name of the Lord thy God in vain" (EXODUS 20:7). The first rule is, put God first; the second is, get the right picture of God; the third is, think about God in the right way. What a person thinks about determines what he is. Hawthorne tells about the boy Ernest who would look longingly at the great stone face on the side of the mountain. It was a strong, kind, honorable face that thrilled the heart of this boy. There was a legend that some day a man would appear who would look like the Great Stone Face. Through all his childhood, and even after he became a man, Ernest kept looking at the great face and for the man who was like it. One day, when the people were discussing the legend, someone suddenly cried out, "Behold, behold, Ernest is himself the likeness of the Great Stone Face." Indeed he was; he had become like his thoughts.

The secret desires of our hearts eventually show up in our very appearance. Once someone wanted Lincoln to meet a certain man. "I do not want to see him," Lincoln said. But his friend protested, "You do not even know him." Lincoln replied, "I do not like his face." "A man cannot be held responsible for his face," the friend said. "Any grown man is responsible for the look on his face," the president insisted.

And Lincoln was right. His own face was an example. Though homely and rough, in Lincoln's face one sees the very principles of sympathy and honesty which made him the greatest of all Americans.

Some psychologists have made extensive studies which show that a person's thoughts show up in his features. I have noticed that married couples who have lived together happily and harmoniously over a number of years come to look more like brother and sister than like husband and wife. As they live together, enjoy common experiences, think alike, they tend to look alike.

Ralph Waldo Emerson, one of the wisest of Americans, said, "A man is what he thinks about all day long." But that was not original with him. Marcus Aurelius, the wisest man of ancient Rome, said, "Our life is what our thoughts make of it." But before Aurelius said it, the wise men of the Bible said, "For as he thinketh in his heart, so is he" (PROVERBS 23:7).

Once a football coach was worried because one of his boys who was capable of being a really great player was not showing up well. The coach decided to go to the boy's room one night and have a talk with him. There on the walls he saw a number of lewd and immoral pictures, and then he understood. No boy could fill his mind with filth and trash and give his best performance on the field of play.

God's third rule is that we put something high and holy in our thinking to reverence, to be inspired by.

St. Paul tells us: "Whatsoever things are true . . . honest . . . just . . . pure . . . lovely . . . of good report . . . think on these things" (PHILIPPIANS 4:8). Those are qualities of God. As we think of Him, it lifts and inspires our lives and make us Godly.

There are at least three ways we profane God's name. First, by our language. We have all kinds of maniacs but one of the most common types we have in America is "swearomaniacs." It is alarming how our language is being filled with profanity. Many of our modern novels I would enjoy reading, but they contain such vile language that I will not read them because I do not want those words in my mind. The word "hell" has become one of our most common words. We say, "It is cold as hell," "It is hot as hell," "It is raining like hell," etc., etc. One man came in to see me recently who I thought used the word correctly. He said, "Preacher, I am in a helluva shape," and he was. Hell is down, not up, and to fill my mind with hell and the language of hell degrades my very soul. The word "profane" comes from two Latin words—"pro" meaning in front of and "fane" meaning temple. A profane word is one you would not use in church, and that is a mighty good way to judge the language we use.

Second, we take God's name in vain by not taking Him seriously. We admit there is a God, but our belief is merely lip service. Jesus said, "Whosoever heareth these sayings of mine, and doeth them . . ."

(MATTHEW 7:24). To talk about God and not to live like God is profanity worse than vile language. Belief that does not make a radical difference in life is mere sham and hyprocrisy. As Elton Trueblood put it, "An empty, meaningless faith may be worse than none."

A third way we take God's name in vain is by refusing His fellowship and His help. If I say a man is my friend, yet never want to be with him and do not call on him when I need his help, then I am lying when I use the word "friend." If I believe in a mechanic, then I will go to him when my car needs attention. If I believe in a physician, I will call him when I become sick. Yet, when Adam and Eve sinned, they ran and hid from God. Their descendants have been doing likewise ever since.

On our lives is the stain of sin. There is only One who can forgive sin, and to refuse to pray, to close our Bibles, to turn our backs on the altar of His church is profanity of the worst sort. Once, when I was a little boy, I saw a soft-drink truck which seemed unattended. I slipped one of the bottles in a pocket, and when I got around the bend of the road opened it. The driver stepped up just then and demanded payment, but I had no nickel. He sternly said, "Get the money for me in thirty minutes or I will put you in jail."

I ran home to my father and told him what I had done. He neither condemned nor humiliated me. My own wrong had done that. Instead, he gave me a nickel and quietly said, "Go, pay the man." That is a picture of God. We do wrong and our very conscience condemns us to a hell from which we cannot escape. Then we remember, "If we confess our sins, he is faithful and just to forgive us our sins, and to cleanse us from all unrighteousnes" (1 JOHN 1:9). Humbly we bow before Him and receive His forgiveness. Then we live for Him and according to His ways. That is belief that is not in vain.

IV

REMEMBER THE SABBATH DAY TO KEEP IT HOLY

REMEMBER THE SABBATH DAY, TO KEEP IT HOLY.
SIX DAYS SHALT THOU LABOUR, AND DO ALL THY WORK:
BUT THE SEVENTH IS THE SABBATH OF THE LORD
THY GOD: IN IT THOU SHALT NOT DO ANY WORK, THOU,
NOR THY SON, NOR THY DAUGHTER, THY MANSERVANT,
NOR THY MAIDSERVANT, NOR THY CATTLE, NOR
THY STRANGER THAT IS WITHIN THY GATES: FOR IN
SIX DAYS THE LORD MADE HEAVEN AND EARTH, THE
SEA, AND ALL THAT IN THEM IS, AND RESTED THE
SEVENTH DAY: WHEREFORE THE LORD BLESSED THE
SABBATH DAY, AND HALLOWED IT

EACH ONE OF GOD'S TEN RULES FOR LIVING ARE vital, but in giving them to Moses, God said more about the fourth than any other. God needed only four words in regard to killing, but He used ninety-four words to tell us to "remember the sabbath day, to keep it holy." In the first place, God tells us to remember. In a scientific sense, one never forgets anything. Every thought we have is registered forever on our minds, but, practically, we can forget almost everything. We forget dates and names, we forget duties and even God. Some things we forget on purpose because the remembrance of them is not pleasant. Other things we forget because our minds are preoccupied with other matters. We forget to keep God's day. But God says man needs to set aside a day each week to keep it holy, and to fail to keep that day holy is to suffer.

In the first place, God gave to man the Sabbath as a reward for his labor. The man who labors deserves to rest, and to forget God's gift is only to cheat ourselves.

In his book, *East River,* Sholem Asch quotes the words of an old Jew, Moshe Wolf, in regard to the Lord's day. It is about the best statement on keeping the Sabbath I know. He said: "When a man labors not for a livelihood, but to accumulate wealth, then he is a slave. Therefore it is that God granted the Sabbath. For it is by the Sabbath that we know that we are not working animals, born to eat and to labor. We are men. It is the Sabbath which is man's goal; not labor, but the rest which he earns from his labor. It was because the Jews made the Sabbath holy to God that they were redeemed from slavery in Egypt. It was by the Sabbath that they proclaimed that they were not slaves, but free men."

Second, God gave us Sunday because every man needs to be re-created. Just as a battery can run down and need to be recharged, so can a person. Gerald Kennedy tells of two parties that started out across the plains in the pioneer days, going west to California. One was led by a religious man and one was led by an irreligious man. One group stopped all of each Lord's day for worship and rest. The other party was so anxious to reach the gold of California that it would not take time to stop. The men drove every day. The amazing thing is that the party which observed the

Sabbath arrived first. We have now well established the fact in our own nation that one can do more work in six days, even in five, than in seven. A run-down person is an unproductive person.

Also, we need to re-create our souls. A group of American explorers went to Africa. They employed some native guides. The first day they rushed, as they did also on the second, third, and every day. On the seventh day they noticed the guides sitting under a tree. "Come on," they shouted. One of the guides replied, "We no go today. We rest today to let our souls catch up with our bodies." For that purpose, God says, "Remember the Sabbath."

We have spent so much time arguing about what we should not do on Sunday that we sometimes forget what we should do. God gave us the day, not as a time of prohibitions but rather to give us opportunity for the finest and most important things of life. An old miner once explained to a visitor, "I let my mules spend one day a week outside the mines to keep them from going blind." And the person who does not spend time away from the daily grind of life goes blind in his soul. The philosopher Santayana tells us, "A fanatic is one who, having lost sight of his aim, redoubles his effort." And much of the feverish haste we see today is by aimless, purposeless people. God says we need a day a week to keep our aim. Or, as Carlyle put it, "The man who does not habitually worship is but a pair of spectacles behind which there is no eye."

As a pastoral counselor, I have seen many people who had lost their nerve control. Life for many had become a miserable experience. But it is rare, very rare, to find an uncontrolled person who regularly worships God and keeps His day holy. We have a slang expression, "That got my goat." That phrase had an interesting beginning. Owners of sensitive, high-strung race horses used to keep a goat in the stalls with the horses. The very presence of the calm, relaxed goat helped the horses to relax. On the day before an important race, rival owners would sometimes steal another owner's goats. Thus the horse would not run its best the next day.

Well, we get sensitive and high-strung, and thus we falter in the race of life. Man needs relaxed re-creation and spiritual inspiration. Oliver Wendell Holmes said: "I have in my heart a small, shy plant called reverence; I cultivate that on Sundays." And well it will be if we all cultivate the plant of reverence within our hearts, because, as Dostoevski reminds us, "A man who bows down to nothing can never bear the burden of himself." Many of our fears, worries, and nervous tensions would be saved if we kept this fourth rule of God.

We are in too big a hurry, and we run by far more than we catch up with. The Bible tells us to "be still, and know that I am God" (PSALM 46:10). Beauty doesn't shout. Loveliness is quiet. Our finest moods are not clamorous. The familiar appeals of the Divine are always in calm tones, a still, small voice. Here is the New Testament picture of Jesus: "Behold, I stand at the door, and knock: if any man hear my voice, and open the door, I will come in to him, and will sup with him, and he with me" (REVELATION 3:20). The Divine is not obtrusive. He bursts in on no one's life unbidden. He is reserved and courteous. "We need a day when we can hear such a voice as His. A day when we give the Highest a hearing," as Dr. Fosdick so well said.

Just as men build telescopes to gain a clearer view of the stars, so almost since the dawn of civilization, have men built churches and set aside a day to worship, in order to gain a clearer view of God and the high purposes of life. "Remember the sabbath day, to keep it holy," said God.

V

HONOR THY FATHER AND THY MOTHER

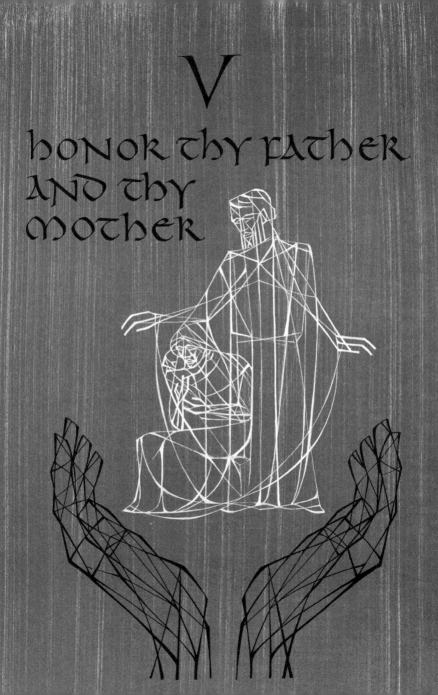

GOD GAVE us ten rules to live by. The first
four deal with our relationship to Him. The last five
deal with our relationship with other people. The
fifth rule has been called the centerpiece of God's
law. "Honour thy father and thy mother" involves
both our relationship with God and with our fellow
men. When God made man He also set up the pat-
tern by which men must live together. First, a man
and a woman come together in marriage, and out of
the union come children. The parents provide love,
care, and control for the child, and, in reality, the
parent is to the child its first god. As the child learns
to love and respect its parents, so later does it love and
respect God.

Also, the parents are the greatest social influence
on the life of the child. It is in the home that a child
first learns to respect the personalities of others, to
have regard for the rights of others, to learn obedience
to the laws for the welfare of all people. A child's
respect for both authority and democracy usually must
begin, if it begins at all, in the home. So, upon the
parent and child relationship in the home rests almost
our entire civilization.

Of course, the relationship of the parent and child
is an ever changing one. At first, the baby must be

carried. Later, it learns to walk, holding its mother's hand; still later, it learns to walk alone. Up to about ten the child thinks its parents know everything. At about sixteen the child is not so sure about its parents. At nineteen the child feels it has surpassed the parents in knowledge and at twenty-two he completely outgrows the parent. But at thirty we remember that our parents were right about a lot of things, and at forty we decide they were just about perfect. That is usually about the normal process.

As I study this rule of God to honor our parents, to me it means three things:

(1) It means that the parents must be honorable. Once a mother carried her little boy to the zoo. He was asking about each of the animals, and when he saw some little ones in a cage, he asked, "What are those?" The mother told him they were little wildcats. He then asked, "Why are they wild cats?" We know the answer. Their mamas and papas were wildcats. Usually, children are the reflection of their parents, because it is the most natural thing for a child so to reverence its parents that it will live according to the principles it sees in them.

When Quentin Roosevelt was on the Western Front during World War I, an observer said, "I come here especially to tell you how millions of Americans appreciate the splendid way in which the sons of Theodore Roosevelt are acquitting themselves in this conflict." "Well, you see," Quentin replied, "it's up to us to practice what Father preaches. I'm Roosevelt's son. It's up to me to live like a Roosevelt."

General Douglas MacArthur expressed the thought I have when he said: "By profession I am a soldier and take pride in that fact. But I am prouder to be a father. My hope is that my son, when I am gone, will remember me not from battle, but in the home, repeating with him one simple prayer, 'Our Father which art in heaven.'"

That is the first meaning of this rule for living which God gave us.

(2) To "honour thy father and thy mother" means not only that parents should be honorable, it means also that children should recognize, respect, and love their parents. It seems to me that just common decency would cause us to honor our parents. Once, when I was pastor of a little country church, I was out visiting and saw a woman picking cotton. I stopped and went down in the field to speak to her. She told me her son had been offered a job in the nearby furniture factory, which would pay good wages, and that she had said to him, "Son, since your father died, I have been working this field to support you in school. You lack just one more year now, and I can keep on so you can finish."

Her hands were rough and calloused, her face was weatherbeaten and her back was stooped, but as that boy looks at her, if he does not feel she is the most beautiful woman in all the world, then he is utterly unworthy of her. Maybe our parents made some mistakes, but they gave us life, they nurtured us as babies, and they loved us, which is more, far more, than anyone else has done or ever can do.

(3) But this rule of life includes more than our immediate parents. It means that we must recognize our debt to the past and be thankful for it. As I stand in my pulpit each Sunday, I am proud to be there. But as I look at the congregation I see men and women who have been there for forty, fifty, and even sixty years. For nearly a hundred years, consecrated people have worked to build the church in which I preach. Back of that is upwards of two thousand years of Christian history, "in spite of dungeon, fire and sword." And still beyond are the prophets of old of Abraham's faith. All the chance and opportunity I have come from the contributions of others better than I. So nothing I could ever do would be equal to what has been done for me.

So many things came crowding in on me the night my father died. I thought of the struggle of his youth to get what little education he could, and the even greater struggle to give his children a better chance than he had. I thought of how as a little boy I went with him to his country churches, and how proud of him I was as he preached. Of how that after I became a preacher I would preach for him and he for me. And now his voice was still. My first feeling of loneliness was overcome by the realization that now I had not only my own work to do, but also his to carry on. Sometimes people tell me I attempt to do too much, but I am caught up by the conviction that I must do the work of two men.

So it is with all of us. What we have and what we are is because of what we have received. We must not only be vessels in which our heritage is carried to the next generations, we must increase that wealth. Each of us is an investment. Our responsibilities differ in that to some have been given five talents, to others two, and to others one. But to take what we have received, be it little or much, and to fail to increase it, is to become a "wicked and slothful servant."

Faith of our fathers, we will love
Both friend and foe in all our strife;
And preach thee, too, as love knows how,
By kindly words and virtuous life:
Faith of our fathers, holy faith,
We will be true to thee till death.

—FREDERICK W. FABER

VI

THOU SHALT NOT KILL

GOD MADE US TO LIVE WITH EACH OTHER, AND THE very process of living requires certain rules. Without rules to go by, the process of living together would be impossible. Here is a highway over which many cars can travel safely if they obey such rules as driving on the right side, not passing except with proper clearance, maintaining a reasonable speed, etc. To break the rules makes the highway unsafe for all who use it, and, instead of an instrument of service, the highway becomes an instrument of death and destruction. Now, life can be good or bad—it depends on how well we keep the rules as we go along. God laid down five rules to govern our relationships with each other. The first one is: "Thou shalt not kill" (EXODUS 20:13).

First, this applies to our own selves. We did not create our lives, and we do not have the authority to destroy our lives. The very fact of life carries with it an inescapable obligation to live. Frequently the question of suicide comes up. Clearly, it is a violation of God's law. Now as to what God does about one who so breaks His law I gladly leave to Him, and I do not know what the eternal result is. God reserves the judgment for Himself, and surely He takes into account all the circumstances and one's mental responsibility.

Not only suicide, but murder, too, is prohibited. All sensible and sane people agree we should not take a

36

gun and shoot either ourselves or another person. But involved in this rule are the laws of health; to violate them is to kill, even though it may be by degrees. This commandment forbids exposing ourselves or others to needless physical risks, such as excessive speed on the highways, unsafe working conditions, improper housing, harmful pleasures, and the like.

Also forbidden is exposing ourselves or others to needless moral or spiritual risks. We can kill by killing faith or ideals. In talking about a man who had leaped from the window of a high building, an old Negro janitor who knew the man's life very wisely said, "When a man has lost God, there ain't nothing to do but jump." Jotham was a king who did not go to church. Being a strong man, he still remained morally upright. But others, seeing his example, did not go either. The result was, "And the people did yet corruptly" (II CHRONICLES 27:2). Also, such things as ingratitude, neglect, cruelty, indifference can be slow but sure instruments of death.

Also forbidden are the destructive emotions of men: fear, hate, jealousy, anger, envy, anxiety, excessive grief, and the others. To counteract them requires developing within our lives the healing and life-giving emotions, such as faith, hope, laughter, creativeness, and love. Love, for example, is a process of giving; giving through love destroys selfishness, which in turn results in the destruction of wrong desire, which in turn results in the destruction of

37

jealousy, which in turn results in the end of hate, which in turn will eliminate the hate murders.

It is a very involved process, not nearly as simple as I state it here. But take excessive grief, for another example. That is a form of self-pity, which grows out of selfishness, which is the lack of outgoing love. "Thou shalt not kill" involves the entire realm of living and the reasons for life. To reverence the life of all men is God's law for us.

To live and let live is only half the meaning of "Thou shalt not kill." Positively, it means to live and help live. Jesus did not find it necessary to warn us against becoming gangsters and murderers, but very clearly does He condemn those who pass by on the other side of a wounded brother. The very foundation of this commandment is the fact that God values every man as He values me. One God who hath made of one blood all nations. One God who is the Father and all men who are brothers. The rule of living means that we look at all men in the proper light.

Lorado Taft, in setting up a statue of a boy by Donatello, put some lights around it. First, he had them down on the floor shining up on the boy's face. As he stepped back and looked at it he was shocked—the boy looked like a moron. He changed the lights. He tried every arrangement. Finally, he put them up above, until they came down on the boy's face. Then he stood back and smiled, for the boy looked like an angel.

That is a wonderful story. When you look at men from merely the earthly level, some do look like morons. Others look inferior, and it is so easy to feel, "Those people do not matter." But when we look at man—any man—through the eyes of the Christian faith, with the light streaming down on him from God, then you see the divinity in him. All life becomes sacred, and you say, "I must not kill—I must help to live."

One of the high moments of *Quo Vadis* is in the arena at night. Queen Lygia has been captured in the early days of Christianity and brought to Rome. Also, her servant Ursus, a giant. Both are Christians and are to be fed to the lions. Their hour comes, thousands are in the arena, and the giant Ursus is led to the center. He kneels in prayer and intends to stay on his knees, offering no resistance. Then dashes in a wild bull, with Lygia the object of his fury.

Seeing the danger of his queen, Ursus seizes the horns of the bull. It is a tremendous struggle, brute strength is pitted against the strength and heart of the giant. Slowly the feet of each sinks into the sand and then slowly the head of the bull begins to go down. In the quietness the people hear the cracking of the bones in the bull's neck as Ursus breaks it. Gently Ursus frees his queen and carries her to safety.

That is the positive side of living. Such beasts as hate, greed, prejudice, war, ignorance, poverty, disease, leave us unmoved until they endanger someone we love. It is then we exert all our strength against them.

And as we come to love all men, so we enter the war against all enemies of men.

One thing more. I know a man who, though well past seventy years, is spending the major portion of his energy in helping to build a school. He told me that he would never be able to see many of the children who would be blessed by his school, but he knew they would be coming and he wanted to prepare for them. That same man is concerned about the conservation of natural resources, about every matter which will make life fuller for the next generation. So much concerned that he gives himself for—

The day in whose clear-shining light,
All wrong shall stand revealed,
When justice shall be clothed with might,
And every hurt be healed.
—FREDERICK L. HOSMER

VII

THOU SHALT NOT COMMIT ADULTERY

FOR A MINISTER TO SPEAK ON THE SEVENTH COM-
mandment—"Thou shalt not commit adultery"—requires unusual tact and reverence, lest even his
rebukes should be like the lights of the Pharos, which
sometimes helped to wreck the vessels they were
meant to save. It is a sin which should be discussed
as little as possible, but, since God lists it in serious-
ness next to murder, and since a large area of our
modern society tends to consider it more a harmless
moral breach than a breaking of God's eternal law,
we need to be reminded that God says, "Thou shalt
not. . . ."

Morris Wee tells that one day his theological professor said to the class, "About fifty per cent of all
human misery is caused by the violation of this commandment." That seems an extreme statement—
"About fifty per cent. . . ." The students did not
believe it, but after a score of years in the ministry,
Dr. Wee says he now knows it is so. Sit with me in
my study in a church on a main thoroughfare of a
great city. Listen to my telephone, read my mail, talk
with many who come in person. You, too, will begin
to believe the professor was right.

Let me ask three questions which I shall try to
answer: What is adultery? Why is it wrong? What
can one who has violated the law do about it?

Adultery is violation of the marriage vow of faithfulness to each other. Any sex experience outside the marriage bond is adultery. Jesus goes even further and says lust in our hearts, even though unexpressed, is adultery (MATTHEW 5:27, 28). We know that sometimes wrong thoughts slip into the mind and we cannot help it, but to turn that thought into lust means to keep it in the mind, secretly to enjoy it, to make friends with it.

It is wrong because God said it is wrong. He said it is wrong because it hurts people. Any person who has any conscience at all feels a deep sense of guilt over the violation of this law. People have told me of stealing and justifying it to the point where they feel they have done no wrong. A man can even commit murder under certain circumstances and not feel he has done wrong. But I have never had one person name the sin of adultery and seek to justify it. We know it is wrong, and there is no circumstance under which it can be justified. Thus, having broken the law, our mind becomes wounded. David's reaction to the transgression of this law is universal: "My sin is ever before me" (PSALM 51:3).

It is wrong because it brings further wrong. A wound in the mind is like a wound in the body. Cut a finger and it won't hurt much, but if the cut becomes infected, the infection will get into the bloodstream, course through the body and eventually kill one. Sorrow is a wound. It cuts deeply and hurts terribly, but it is a clean wound, and unless bitterness,

43

resentment or self-pity gets into the wound, it will heal. But when I do wrong the result is an unclean wound, which will not heal. It robs me of my peace of mind, it makes my conscience hurt, it distorts my thinking, it sets up conflicts within me, it weakens my will power, it destroys my soul.

Phillips Brooks said, "Keep clear of concealment, keep clear of the need of concealment. It is an awful hour when the first necessity of hiding anything comes. When there are eyes to be avoided and subjects which must not be touched, then the whole bloom of life is gone."

The main reason adultery is wrong is that it destroys marriage. You remember the lovely scene in the story, *Mrs. Miniver*. They had just acquired a new car and she also had a new hat. When they go to bed that night they are not sleepy but are thinking of their good fortune. Mrs. Miniver says, "We are the luckiest people." Her husband asks, "Why, because of the new car or the new hat?" "No dear, it is because we have each other." For a happy marriage, a lot of things are not necessary. Money and the things that money can buy are good to have but can be done without. But in marriage there are two things which must exist. First, a solid affection, a love for each other entirely different from the love for anyone else. Second, complete trust in each other. Adultery destroys both.

Beautiful was the custom of the Cherokee Indians. In the marriage ceremony the couple would join hands across a running stream to signify that forever their lives would flow together.

Suppose one is guilty of adultery; can anything be done about it? Turn to the eighth chapter of St. John's Gospel and read there how a guilty one was brought before Jesus. The crowd had no solution but to stone her. They asked Jesus' opinion. His solution to any wrong never was stoning. He hated the sin but He never ceased to love the sinner.

When I was a little boy living in Tate, Georgia, I once was deeply impressed with a story I heard Mr. Sam Tate tell. There was an habitual drunkard in the community, and one morning he said, "Sam, the boys rocked me last night." "Maybe they were trying to make a better man out of you," replied Mr. Tate. "Well," the poor fellow said, "I never heard of Jesus throwing rocks at a man to make him better."

In the midst of the crowd with the guilty woman before Him, Jesus said nothing. Instead, He stooped down and began writing on the ground. I wonder what He wrote. After a while, He spoke softly, yet so all could hear, "He that is without sin among you, let him cast the first stone." Again He stooped down and wrote on the ground. Perhaps He knew that crowd of self-righteous people who were always ready to push somebody further down. My guess is He wrote such words as "liar," "thief," "hypocrite." One by one, the men who were so ready to condemn dropped their rocks and shamefacedly slipped away.

45

Now comes one of the grandest scenes in the entire Bible. The matchless Saviour is alone with the woman. Not one harsh word comes from His lips. Not even a look of rebuke. Instead, gently and tenderly He says, "Neither do I condemn thee: go, and sin no more." In my mind I see her as she stands. She rises to her full height, her chin goes up and her shoulders back as the burden of her soul is lifted. She is caught up in the power of new self-respect and another chance.

Tradition has it that it was she who stood by Mary, the virgin mother, at the foot of the cross that day. Also, that it was she who first received the message of His resurrection and was given the blessed privilege of telling others. To announce His birth, God sent His angels from heaven. That privilege was not given to mortal man. But to tell of His living again, this fallen one was selected. Whatever my sin, Christ, and Christ alone, can take away the guilt and let me live again.

VIII

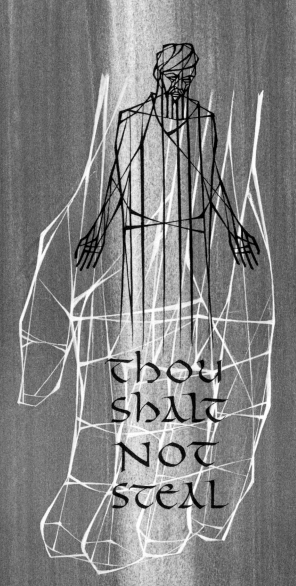

thou
shalt
not
steal

GOD's EIGHTH RULE FOR LIFE, "THOU SHALT NOT steal," is the foundation of our entire economic system, because it recognizes the fact that one has a right, a God-given right, to work, earn, save, and own. To take away from one that which is rightfully his is wrong in the sight of God. In the creation story we are told how God made the earth, the sea and everything on the earth and in the sea. Then He made man and gave to man dominion over His creation (GENESIS 1:26). Actually, no person owns anything. All belongs to God, but while man is on earth he has the God-given right of possession. To deny any man that right violates the very basis of God's creation.

Since the beginning of time various economic systems have been tried, but only one will really work and that is free enterprise by Godly people. It has been pointed out that the first Christians tried a form of collective ownership, but it also needs to be remembered that their experiment failed and they soon abandoned it. St. Paul writes, "If any would not work, neither should he eat" (II THESSALONIANS 3:10).

Once Jesus told a story of a man who was taking a journey from Jerusalem down to Jericho. He fell among thieves, who robbed and beat him and left him wounded by the roadside. A priest and a Levite came along, saw the man, but passed by on the other side. A Samaritan came along, helped the man, and made

48

financial provision for his keep while he could not care for himself (LUKE 10:30, 37). In that simple story we have clearly demonstrated the three possible philosophies of wealth. The interpretation is not original with me.

First, the philosophy of the thieves is: "What belongs to my neighbor belongs to me and I will take it." There is aggressive stealing—by the robber, the embezzler, and all the others. Included also is such a thing as living beyond one's means. To go in debt without a reasonable probability of being able to pay back is stealing. To fail to give an honest day's work is also stealing. Once a servant girl applied for membership in a church, but could give no evidence of her conversion and was about to be sent away. The pastor asked, "Is there no evidence which would indicate a change of heart?" She replied, "Now I don't sweep under the rugs in the house where I am employed." "It is enough," he said, "we will receive her into our fellowship."

Also, we can steal from another his inner supports. One does not live by bread alone. When Mark Twain married Olivia Langdon she was a very devout Christian. He was so unsympathetic with her faith that gradually she gave up her religious practices. Later, there came into her life a very deep sorrow. He urged, "Livy, lean on your faith." Sadly she told him, "I can't. I haven't any left." To his dying day he was haunted by the fact that he had taken from her that which had meant so much.

Shakespeare put his finger on the worst form of stealing when he told us: "He that filches from me my good name robs me of that which not enriches him and makes me poor indeed." Before repeating something bad about another person, ask yourself these three questions: Is it true? Is it necessary for me to tell it? Is it kind to tell it?

There are many ways of aggressive stealing.

Second, not only can we steal by taking from another, we also steal by withholding from our fellows. The philosophy of the priest and Levite in the story of the Good Samaritan was: "What belongs to me is mine and I will keep it." Some people's measure of success is how much they can grab hold of and hold onto. As I go about I see a lot of "coffin" men. They have room for themselves and nobody else. They live in the spirit of the little girl who said:

I gave a little party this afternoon at three;
'Twas very small, three guests in all, just I, myself
*   and me.*
Myself ate up all the sandwiches, while I drank up
*   the tea,*
And it was I who ate the pie, and passed the cake
*   to me.*

Jesus told us of such a man. He was very successful and accumulated more than he needed. What did he do? "I will pull down my barns, and build greater; and there will I bestow all my fruits and my goods." Saving is a virtue, but a very dangerous virtue. Every dollar I possess carries with it a corresponding obligation. This man was so blinded by his greed that he failed to see his opportunities and his obligations. The result was he lost his soul (LUKE 12:16-21).

The prophet Malachi asked the sobering question, "Will a man rob God?" He answers by saying we have robbed God "in tithes and offerings" (MALACHI 3:8). It is a clear law of God that we return unto Him ten percent of all He permits us to possess, and it is a fearful thing to come before Him in judgment with His money that we had kept or used for ourselves.

Third, the Good Samaritan saw his brother's need and his philosophy was "What belongs to me belongs to others, and I will share it." Let us never forget that the right of private enterprise and ownership is not something we have earned. Rather is it our God-given privilege. God expresses His faith in us, but He also demands an accounting. Ability, talents, opportunity, material resources are really not ours. They are God's investments in us. And like any wise investor, God expects dividends. Suppose I put my money into a company, and the officers of the company use all the profits for themselves. I would be cheated. Likewise can we cheat God.

But how can I give to God what is rightfully His? There is only one way; that is in service to others. So, the positive meaning of "Thou shalt not steal" is consecrated service, both of my material resources and of my life. Bernard Shaw once said; "A gentleman is one who puts more into life than he takes out."

One thing more. Once Jesus went home with a man named Zacchaeus. Later on, we hear Zacchaeus saying, "Lord, the half of my goods I give to the poor; and if I have taken any thing from any man . . . I restore him fourfold." Jesus replied, "This day is salvation come to this house" (LUKE 19:8, 9). Stealing demands restitution. No man has room for both Christ and dishonest gains. He must decide between the two. It is often not an easy decision to make. But it may help to decide by asking ourselves, "For what shall it profit a man, if he shall gain the whole world, and lose his own soul?" (MARK 8:36).

IX

THOU SHALT NOT BEAR FALSE WITNESS AGAINST THY NEIGHBOR

OF THE TEN COMMANDMENTS, THE ONE WE BREAK the most is the ninth—"Thou shalt not bear false witness against thy neighbour." One reason for this is that we talk most about people. Those of great minds discuss ideas, people of mediocre minds discuss events, and those of small minds discuss other people. Most of us have never made much mental development. Another reason we break this commandment is because it ministers to our own pride. It takes some of the sting out of our own failures if we can rub off the glitter of someone else's crown. It is a sure sign of an inferiority complex when a person tells of the faults of another. Back of much gossip is jealousy.

However, hardly anybody feels guilty of violating this law. I have had people confess to me the breaking of every one of the Ten Commandments except this one. I have never heard a person admit gossiping. We say, "I don't mean to talk about him, but . . ." and off we go. We assume a self-righteous attitude which we feel gives us license to condemn sin. But all the time we enjoy talking about the sin and, in a back-handed way, brag of ourselves because we have not done exactly what the person we are telling about has done.

Sometimes our gossip takes the form of a false sympathy. "Isn't it too bad how Mr. Blank beats his wife?

I am so sorry for her." Or maybe we just ask a question. "Is it true that Mr. and Mrs. Blank are on the verge of divorce?" That is the method of the devil. He would not accuse Job of any wrongdoing. Instead, he merely asked, "Doth Job fear God for nought?" (JOB 1:9). The mere question raises a suspicion as to Job's sincerity.

Then we gossip just by listening. There cannot be a noise unless there is an ear to hear it. A noise is caused by the vibrations of the ear drums. And neither can there be a bit of gossip without an ear to hear. The law holds the receiver of stolen goods as guilty as the thief. It is really an insult to you for someone to tell you of the vices of another man, because in so doing he is passing judgment, not only on the subject of his gossip, but also on you. If someone tells you a dirty joke, his very action is saying that he thinks of you as one interested in dirty jokes. For one to tell you of another's sins means that the gossiper's opinion of you is that you would be glad to know such things. It is really an insult to you.

Usually we do not mean to hurt others whom we talk about. We think of talebearing as a bit of harmless pastime. But let us remember the words of our Lord, "Judge not, that ye be not judged. For with what judgment ye judge, ye shall be judged: and with what measure ye mete, it shall be measured to you again" (MATTHEW 7:1, 2). That statement scares me. It drives me to my knees. I want God to be kinder toward me than I have been toward others. Don't you?

"So live," advised Will Rogers, "that you would not be ashamed to sell the family parrot to the town gossip." That is good advice, but I am afraid not many of us have lived up to it. Therefore, we should remind ourselves of the old saying:

> *There is so much good in the worst of us,*
> *And so much bad in the best of us,*
> *That it ill behooves the best of us,*
> *To talk about the rest of us.*

A modern translation of Jesus' words in Matthew 7:5 is: "Thou hypocrite, first cast out the two by four out of thine own eye; and then shalt thou see clearly to cast out the splinter out of thy brother's eye."

Whenever I think of the ninth commandment, "Thou shalt not bear false witness," I am haunted by a story which Pierre Van Paassen tells in his book, *The Days of Our Years.* I have seen the story quoted in many places, but would like to tell it briefly again. There was a hunchback by the name of Ugolin who fell sick. He never knew his father, and his mother was a drunken outcast. He had a lovely sister named Solange. Because she loved Ugolin so much and because she could get the money to buy his medicine in no other way, she sold her body on the streets.

People talked so harshly that Ugolin drowned himself in the river, and Solange shot herself. For their funeral the little village church was crowded. The minister mounted the pulpit and began his sermon:

"Christians" [*the word was like a whip-lash*], *"Christians, when the Lord of life and death shall ask me on the Day of Judgment, 'Where are thy sheep?' I shall not answer Him. When the Lord asks me the second time, 'Where are thy sheep?' I will yet not answer Him. But when the Lord shall ask me a third time, 'Where are thy sheep?' I shall hang my head in shame and I will answer Him, 'They were not sheep, Lord, they were a pack of wolves.'"*

In a recent sermon I said the person who talks about one who sins is worse than the one who actually commits the sin. That is a rather extreme statement which I made extemporaneously in an off-guarded moment. I am not sure it is true. Yet I am not sure it isn't true. What do you think? Before you answer, turn over and read the story about Noah getting drunk (GENESIS 9:20, 27).

Noah was a preacher. Now, it is shameful for any person to get drunk, but for one who wears the royal purple of the prophet it is a double shame. Noah lay in his tent disgracefully naked. After a while his son Ham came and saw his father and he went out and told it. Noah's two other sons, Shem and Japheth, refused to look upon their father. Instead, they backed into the tent and covered their father with a garment.

Many generations later, when the author of Hebrews writes of the great men of faith, he tells of Noah's mighty work and does not remember his fall against him (HEBREWS 11:7). Undoubtedly God forgot it also. Japheth and Shem were blessed of God and they prospered. But Ham, the son who told of his father's nakedness, was cursed and was condemned to the life of a servant. Maybe, after all, he who actually commits the sin comes out better than he who tells about it.

Jim was considered the bad boy of the community. He was blamed for everything. He took his whippings at school without complaint and with no tears. But one year a new schoolteacher came, and when something happened, naturally everyone blamed that boy. He expected the usual beating. Instead, the teacher said, "Now, let Jim tell his side." To the surprise of everyone, Jim began to cry. When the teacher asked, "What is the matter?" Jim replied, "This is the first time anybody ever said I had a side."

One of my favorite verses of Scripture is: "Brethren, if a man be overtaken in a fault, ye which are spiritual, restore such a one in the spirit of meekness; considering thyself, lest thou also be tempted" (GALATIANS 6:1).

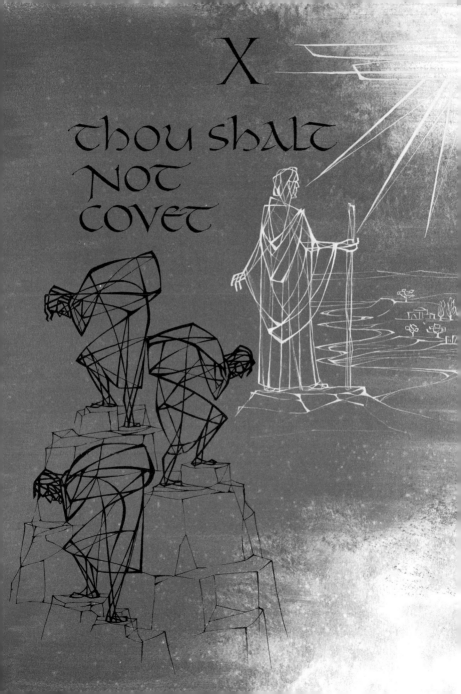

THOU SHALT NOT COVET THY NEIGHBOUR'S HOUSE,
THOU SHALT NOT COVET THY NEIGHBOUR'S WIFE,
NOR HIS MANSERVANT, NOR HIS MAIDSERVANT,
NOR HIS OX, NOR HIS ASS, NOR ANY THING THAT IS
THY NEIGHBOUR'S

GOD'S FINAL RULE FOR LIFE IS, "THOU SHALT NOT covet." Of course, that do not mean that all desire is wrong. Without desires, no one would have any ambition, we would not work, we would not make progress. To covet means that I think of myself and of what I can get. God would have us forget ourselves and think of what we can give. This same command- ment is stated by Jesus in a positive way. St. Paul quotes Him as saying, "It is more blessed to give than to receive" (ACTS 20:35).

The word "covet" comes from a Greek word which means "grasping for more." No matter how much one gets, he is always discontented, and eventually, after covetousness drives him unmercifully through life, it kills him and leaves him with nothing. Tolstoy told a story which illustrates the activity of covetousness. A peasant was offered all the land he could walk around in a day. So the man started, hurrying to get around as much as possible. But the exertion he put forth was so great that he fell dead just as he got back to where he had begun. He ended up with nothing.

God gave these ten laws for our good. He wants us to be our very best and to get the most that is possible out of life. His last rule brings us to the very climax of living, which is contentment. That is what we all want. Contentment gives peace and joy in our minds and hearts, which is the reward of living God's way. But this must be the last of the ten rules. Without the other nine, it is impossible to observe. How does one root out of his life wrong desire? It is by filling his life with right desires.

The best summary of the Ten Commandments is the one Jesus gave: "Thou shalt love the Lord thy God with all thy heart, and with all thy soul, and with all thy mind. . . . Thou shalt love thy neighbour as thyself" (MATTHEW 22:37, 39). Put God and others first, get something into your mind greater than yourself. In so doing you lose yourself, selfishness is blotted out; instead of making ourselves miserable by what we do not have, we begin to gain the blessed thrill of giving what we can give.

There is a good story of four men who climbed a mountain. The first complained that his feet hurt. The second had a greedy eye and kept wishing for each house and farm he could see. The third saw clouds and was worried for fear that it might rain. But the fourth fixed his eyes on the marvelous view. In looking away from himself and from the valley below, the little worries which made the others so unhappy were unnoticed.

And when in our view appears the vision of God and of opportunities of service to our fellow men, we experience, not misery-giving selfishness, but the fruits of the spirit. In losing our selfish desires, we gain love, joy, peace, long-suffering, gentleness, goodness, faith, meekness, and temperance. Those are the fruits of the spirit, the results of living God's way (GALATIANS 5:22, 23).

As we study the Ten Commandments we become almost overwhelmed by a sense of guilt and of shame. We have not lived up to God's rules; in so many places have we failed.

I do not know what the final Judgment Day of God is like. We have a mental picture of Him sitting as the judge with a big book before Him in which are listed all our transgressions. Maybe it will not be that way at all. However, one thing we know; there will be a judgment. How will you plead? Did you worship idols in the place of God?—Guilty! Did you fail to live up to your highest belief, profane God's name, pay no respect to His day?—Guilty! Were you untrue to the best of the past, did you fail to support life as you might have done, were you dishonest and unclean?— Guilty! Did you bear false witness, have evil desire?— Guilty!

As we think of tomorrow we are painfully conscious of our inadequacy and our inability to live as we should. We almost give up to hopelessness and despair. Then we think of something else—the greatest something which can occupy a human mind. Let me give here a story of which Morris Wee reminds us.

As a young man, Dr. A. J. Cronin was in charge of a small hospital. One evening he performed an emergency operation on a little boy. It was a very delicate operation, and the doctor felt great relief when the little fellow breathed freely after it was over. He gave orders to the young nurse and went home filled with gratitude for the success. Late that night came a frantic call for the doctor. Everything had gone wrong, and the child was in desperate condition. When Dr. Cronin got to the bedside the boy was dead.

The nurse had become frightened and had neglected her duty. Dr. Cronin decided she should not be trusted again, and he wrote a letter to the board of health which would end her career as a nurse. He called her in and read the letter to her. She listened in shame and misery, saying nothing. Finally, Dr. Cronin asked, "Have you nothing to say?" She shook her head. She had no excuse to offer. Then she did speak, and this is what she said: "Give me another chance."

God gave us these ten rules to live by. Surely His heart has been grieved as again and again we violated them. We stand before Him in shame and misery, condemned without excuse. Not because we deserve it, but because of His infinite mercy, God gives us another chance. "For God so loved the world, that he gave his only begotten Son, that whosoever believeth in him should not perish, but have everlasting life" (JOHN 3:16).

If you have not broken one of God's commandments, I suppose you do not need the Saviour. But is there one among us who is innocent? We can only sing: "Just as I am, without one plea, but that Thy blood was shed for me." And as we look to the future we triumphantly say with the Apostle, "I can do all things through Christ which strengtheneth me" (PHILIPPIANS 4:13). Through faith in Christ and obedience to His will our sins are forgiven and we have strength for victory tomorrow.